Jesus' Belief in Man

Jesus'

"Seeing the crowds, he went up on the mountain, and when he sat down his disciples came to him. And he opened his mouth and taught them."

Matt. 5:1-2

"Thither our path lies; wind we up the heights;
   Wait ye the warning?
Our low life was the level's and the night's;
   He's for the morning."

Robert Browning

Belief in Man

Edwin McNeill Poteat

ABINGDON PRESS
NEW YORK • NASHVILLE

UNITY SCHOOL LIBRARY
DISCARD
Lee's Summit, Missouri 64063

JESUS' BELIEF IN MAN

Copyright © MCMLVI by Pierce & Washabaugh

All rights in this book are reserved.
No part of the book may be used or reproduced in any manner whatsoever without written permission of the publishers except brief quotations embodied in critical articles or reviews. For information address Abingdon Press, 810 Broadway, Nashville 2, Tennessee

Library of Congress Catalog Card Number: 56-8743

Scripture quotations unless otherwise designated are from the Revised Standard Version of the Bible and are copyright 1946, 1952 by the Division of Christian Education of the National Council of the Churches of Christ in the United States of America.

SET UP, PRINTED, AND BOUND BY THE
PARTHENON PRESS, AT NASHVILLE,
TENNESSEE, UNITED STATES OF AMERICA

Dedicated

to

WILDA HARDMAN POTEAT

Foreword

Why do we endlessly turn back to a consideration of the nature of man? Perhaps it is because our bred-in egoism will allow us no respite from thinking about ourselves. We are fantastically complex and efficient radioactivated machines. Genes and chromosomes are life's mysterious vehicles of transit from parent to child, past to future. Are we more than that? This is the interest of naturalism.

Or it may be that the ambivalence of our monitory moods, love, faith, hope (we hate what we love, doubt what we believe, despair of what we hope), creates tensions which first demand that they be confronted and then that they be resolved or used constructively. This is the interest of psychology.

Because man stands both within and apart from his natural habitat, he must search for harmony where the time-space and the eternal-infinite cancel each other in soundlessness or collide in disharmony. Thus philosophy asks its questions.

Man feels shame for his folly, guilt for his sin. Is this a pestilence he cannot cure or a persuasion that can guide him into ways of wisdom and righteousness? If he is not helpless, whence comes his help? If he is not doomed, whence his rescue? Thus the domain of theology.

Today we hear of "hollow men," of "faceless men," of the "indifferentiated mass." These are new phrasings of old feelings. Before T. S. Eliot, Job spoke of the "void man"; and before Arthur Koestler, Ecclesiastes knew how the face, outlined by wisdom, could be obscured by ignorance. If man today is empty, what has eviscerated him? If he is losing his identity in the mass, what has erased his features?

These are questions which engage all serious reflections about man and his world. Being egoists we shall continue to puzzle about ourselves and perhaps dissolve our bewilderment alternately in tears and laughter. Despite our fondness for a confident word, when we walk through the valley of the shadow of death, we *will* fear evil. Similarly when we walk along the highway of God, we shall be bold because no lions go up thereon. And every once in a while we will turn back to an ancient record and trace the footsteps of one who knew what it was to be a man. Lao-tzu believed man to be essentially free and good; Gautama believed man to be the prisoner of desire; Israel believed man to be the creative work of Yahweh. What did Israel's greatest Son believe?

Because he still ranges high above the levels of most of our thought and life, we shall once again try to listen for the voice that like a breath from the mountain may still speak to us

> In accents clear and still,
> Above the storms of passion,
> The murmurs of self-will.

EDWIN MCNEILL POTEAT

Contents

I. Introduction 11

II. Sense of Power 18

III. The Integrity of Law 25

IV. Salt, Light, and Beatitude 35

V. Fulfillment of the Law 47

VI. The Fulfillment of Prophecy 61

VII. The Proverbs of Jesus 76

VIII. Man in Society 100

IX. The New and the Old 122

X. Jesus and People 132

XI. Summary and Conclusion 147

CHAPTER I

Introduction

Much has been written about the identity of Jesus and God. Sometimes it takes the form of saying Jesus is God. This is an identity of being and lies in the area of metaphysics. Or it takes the form of saying Jesus is like God or God is like Jesus. This is an identity of function and lies in the area of form or as the philosopher would put it, entelechy.

Less has been written about the identity of Jesus with man. There was once a heresy that split the Church claiming that Jesus' identity with humanity was not real. He had an ethereal or phantom body uncorrupted by matter, which was regarded as essentially evil. Countering this pious effort to emancipate him from elemental impurity was the assertion that he was truly human but withal so impregnated with the divine that he was able to cleanse the corruptions of the flesh and thus be both real and sinless. The generations of reflection on the phenomenon of Jesus have, generally speaking, left us with the not altogether clear formula of his human divinity or divine humanity.

From what Jesus had to say about himself, we are compelled to think that he regarded his relation to the Father more under the aspect of function than of essence. This may be because his reported ideas about himself and God were more practical than philosophical. Certain it is that he is recorded as making much of his identification of himself with God in what he did. The Fourth Gospel, which presents him metaphysically as the Word made flesh (the enfleshment of God), also calls him Son of God, Lamb of God, Messiah, King of Israel, Son of man, Teacher come from God, only begotten Son, Prophet, Rabbi, Savior of the world—most of these are designations of function found within the first four chapters.

When he speaks of himself, he is reticent with titles but explicit about his responsibilities. "My food is to do the will of him who sent me, and to accomplish his work." (John 4:34.) "My Father is working still, and I am working." (John 5:17.) "The Son can do nothing of his own accord . . . ; whatever he does, that the Son does likewise." (John 5:19.) These all clearly represent his sense of identity of vocation. "The testimony which I have is greater than that of John [who had declared him to be the Son of God and Lamb of God, and so on]; for the works which the Father has granted me to accomplish, these very works which I am doing, bear me witness that the Father has sent me." (John 6:36.) Here it was what he was doing that was his "greater" credential.

However unique he may have regarded his work to be, it is clear that he expected his friends to be engaged in the same sort of enterprise. *"We* must work the works of him who sent me." (John 9:4.) "I have given you an example, that you also should do as I have done to you." (John 13:15.) "If you know these things, blessed are you if you do them." (John 13:17.) And he even promised that their labors would surpass his own: "He who believes in me will also do the works that I do; and greater works than these will he do, because I go to the Father" (John 14:12).

Other references from the Synoptics will come readily to mind in support of the proposition that Jesus expressed his sense of identification with God in the works he did and that he also expected the participation of his friends in the works of God. This is to be taken not as blurring the uniqueness of Jesus' incarnational relation to God but as a sharper focus on the identification that Jesus made between himself and his friends. Again I point out that this was a practical rather than a metaphysical identification.

INTRODUCTION

This has, I believe, immense importance for what we are to think about human nature. A biblical doctrine of man is not to be had simply by citing references or constructing a textual trellis. Insofar as it is to be put together from a study of the Gospels, it will be found first in what Jesus thought of himself within the human scene and second in what he said about human behavior. His practical identification of himself with humanity makes what he said about himself relevant to human nature and what he said about human nature relevant to himself. In other words he made no empirical difference between himself and his friends. Their attachment to him was due largely to what he did with and for them, not because they had found him to be an interesting puzzle. He was for them carnate man rather than incarnate Son. The latter designation came many years later, long after his works had ceased and their works (his also) had achieved prodigies in his name.

Paul was one day to write his Corinthian friends that "God was in Christ reconciling the world to himself, . . . and entrusting to us the message of reconciliation" (II Cor. 5:19). This is a further practical identification of Jesus with his followers in the redemptive enterprise, this time at the initiative of God. It is possible then to say, avoiding at this point the pitfalls of metaphysics, that Jesus was like God and that man is like Jesus. This may do violence to the *feeling* we have for the uniqueness of our Lord's relation to the divine Father, but it also gives support to the *feeling* that our human nature is like his and that what he said and did is a demonstration not solely of Godliness but also of humanness.

To be sure, "no man ever spoke like this man!" This self-defense of the bailiffs sent to arrest Jesus did not mean he spoke gibberish or talked about things they couldn't understand. On the contrary. It was because he approached the human scene with such uncomplicated simplicity and spoke

13

of the human predicament so lucidly that they said he was "out of this world."

Similarly, therefore, when we hear him speaking to the human situation, we shall many times marvel at the depths to which he probed and the serenity and confidence with which he exposed the hidden vitalities that lie beneath the surface of ordinary men's lives. But we shall not for that reason think that he was talking to men in terms that were unintelligible because men were a genus different from himself, or that he was laying before them wisdom they could not accept or mandates to which they could not respond because they were unequipped by their nature to do so.

The interest we have in this perspective on the following study of the teachings of Jesus lies primarily in the fact that much thinking about human nature today is corrupted by what are inexactly called both the political left and the theological right. Our concern is not to find a middle ground but to rediscover the biblical ground no matter toward which side it may lean. It has always been important to understand what man is, to have a credible doctrine of man. Never has the necessity been more compelling. It is unfortunate that the note of optimism sounded today about human nature seems to come from Marxism that bases it on foundations unacceptable to the Christian testimony, while the note of pessimism sounded by the prevailing theological trumpeters rests on an understanding of human nature that has no basis in the teaching of the Son of man.

Indeed, save for a few unhappy references in Paul's writings which bespeak less his good judgment than his poor health, the whole Bible has an understanding about humankind that is good-humored without sentimentality and hopeful without vacuity. The Decalogue may be thus understood; for it deals not simply with a creature that can kill, corrupt, steal, and lie but with a man who can protect himself and his fellow in a society that regards life, integrity, property, and justice as basic moral rights. Otherwise the Commandments are a fraud.

I go beyond this to say that the Augustinian misunderstanding of the Genesis record has left an inheritance of error concerning man's sin that is untenable in the light of a modern understanding of Adam's daring and costly self-affirmation in the Garden imbroglio.

This is certainly no time for frothy hilarity about how nice we all are, nor by the same token is it time for emotional heaviness and low spirits. We still live within the ancient religious tradition that was given lift and illumination by good news about both man the individual and man in fellowship. Sons of God in the kingdom of heaven: that was the gospel that created a new world culture. This was not blind to man's silliness and his sin; neither did it regard him as implacably doomed because of an unredeemable something with which he was born. The biblical doctrine of man needs to be restated in an age when cynicism and pessimism have soured and shadowed it. It was with this in view that this study was undertaken.

It is proper that the pattern of the study be anticipated here. The first encounter we have with the adult Jesus shows him entering the world that lay geographically beyond his native town and morally beyond the sheltered piety of a Jewish family. His sense of vocation was clear and compulsive, and it demanded that he think or rethink his relation to the ordered universe within which he was to bear his testimony and work the works of him who had sent him. Again, he had to think or rethink about the human order—or disorder—within which he was so briefly to live. What was man? What could be expected of him? How far is the surface—whether serene or turbulent—to be trusted as a true representation of man's nature? Again, what of the law given for his guidance? Is it fixed or flexible, and what is the permanent element in it? And when men under the constraint of God find themselves in a fellowship called the Kingdom, where is the cohesive center and what is the dynamic of their continuing development together?

These are not all the questions that can be asked, but they are enough to show that there was a pivot about which all inquiry revolved: the nature of man. This is reflected in Jesus and in those with whom he shared his purpose and work. Had our Lord not felt as he clearly did about man's nature ("he knew all men and needed no one to bear witness of man; for he himself knew what was in man" [John 2:25])[1] it would be difficult to account either for what he said or for his flintlike dedication to the redemptive program of his Father.

Thus we shall survey what are familiar to us as the Temptations, the Sermon on the Mount, the parables of the Kingdom, and the First and Great Commandment. These have been the subject of countless treatises, for they are the heart of the Good News. They shall be studied in the effort to distill from them what may be correctly regarded as Jesus' informal formulation of a doctrine of man.

The topography of Palestine is rugged, and its elevations roll and jut above its low valleys. It is not surprising, therefore, that Jesus is often pictured on hillsides or mountain crests. The experiences about which our interest shall center are for the most part related to some eminence to which he, and often his followers, made their way. And as the winds

[1] Three things may be said about this verse: first, that the comment follows an episode in which Jesus is represented as being unwilling to "trust himself to them," meaning those who had believed merely in the signs which he did. This would appear to be an adverse and unflattering judgment, yet it was the very capacity for deep faith that made him unresponsive to shallow faith. Second, the generic use of the word man is significant. Third, it is an effective summary of something that appears on nearly every page of the Gospels, namely, the extraordinary way in which Jesus saw beneath pretense and subterfuge to the essential quality of individual and action.

move restlessly about the shoulders and summits of the uplands, so the words of Jesus forever stir like breath from the mount to restore and refresh man's faith in God and in himself. To try to capture a wisp or to feel the full pressure of this moving air is a responsibility never to be fully discharged but similarly never to be surrendered.

CHAPTER II

Sense of Power

It strains the words too much to call the Gospel records biographies of Jesus. They are fragments, episodes, or constellations of events, memorabilia put together by his friends or friends of his friends. They were constructing a gospel, not a story; it was a beginning ("the beginning of the gospel of Jesus Christ" [Mark 1:1]), not a compendium.

While they are not biography, they contain what is manifestly a brief bit of autobiography—the Temptations—which the writers felt was indispensable to any statement of the Good News. This raises an important question: Why was the report of the temptations of Jesus good news? On the contrary, it could have been regarded as bad news that the forces of evil are so sinister and insatiable that they will even tackle one who has just been fortified by the overwhelming sense of his appointment to divine sonship and the accolade of divine favor. "Thou art my beloved Son; with thee I am well pleased." (Mark 1:11.)

The wilderness experience was solitary and was therefore reported to rather than shared by his friends. Did Jesus see it in relation to an evangel, a recalled event that was to be made part of a body of witness that would point out to humanity the way of salvation? Was it the prototype of everyman's encounter with life? Or did he think that this panorama of fact and fantasy (he could see real stones and the real Temple, but no mountain is high enough to afford a real view of the kingdoms of the world) was uniquely his own and thus set him off from all the sons of men? If not, how was it good news? Where does it fit in a story that was destined to move the world in the direction of the fulfillment of the divine will?

The answer would appear to be found in its dramatization of the sense and the test of power that is basic to everyman's experience of self-affirmation. Since in a manner of speaking consciously self-directed life is simply the use of one's powers, the most significant fact about a man is his awareness of power and the way he uses it.

Jesus had been made aware of power at his baptism. This was the affirmation of God. He was presently to go into the rugged wilderness under the stern compulsions of the Spirit. Denied all the external supports of friendly power—companionship, food, and shelter—and surrounded by what to him must have seemed the portents of hostile power—wild beasts, an inhospitable mountainside, and forty days of privation—he was to pit his naked power against the puissant malevolence of evil. Here, as the grim contest was waged, if God and his angel emissaries were standing by, they were in ambush.

1

Now it is important to note that the assault of the evil one did not take the line of disparaging his power. The adversary might have taunted him that their contest was uneven and mocked him with the certainty of defeat. Nothing is more subtle than this strategem, to make the enemy suspect his own weakness and call off the fight; this is tried wherever there is conflict, and self-defeat thus inflicted is more humiliating than any other sort. No; his power was conceded to him, power to make stone into bread. The question therefore was not whether he had power but how he would use it.

Generally speaking there are three areas within which one will exercise his power: the physical, social, and moral realms. It is immensely reassuring to know that man is neither the product nor must he be the victim of these areas of existence into which he is unwittingly thrust. The measure of man is therefore to be found in the purposes for which he employs his powers and his skill and persistence in their use.

The subtlety of the suggestion that he make a loaf out of stone is seen if we imagine him accepting it. Suppose he had waved his hand, performed a miracle and got bread, and perhaps a cheese and cruse of water, and satisfied a perfectly normal and satiable need. It would have made a pretty tale in the telling and would have excited admiration rather than repugnance. Would it not have been common prudence, justice even, assuming he had the power to bring it off?

The position he took not only protected him from a misuse of power in the physical realm; it extended the sense of power into the realm we call loosely the spiritual. Man's power is ambivalent; he lives in a time-space continuum—the world of the Stone—and in the timeless-spaceless continuum of the Word. Neither is to be escaped in flight to the other, nor is one to resign one's self to impotence in either. We see what happens when power over the physical world completely engrosses man. Today we stand in terror before the uranium "stones" that under the power touch of man thrust titan fists upward into the writhing air. Where is man's power of the Word? What he is doing physically now threatens to erase all the words his culture has written or to silence the words he speaks for God or for himself.

2

But man's sense of power extends beyond the physical world of sticks and stones; he lives in a social world also. Human beings use one another; that is, they employ their power to get things done among and by their fellows. Here the sense of power can be benign or malignant; the opposite impulses to serve and to dominate both spring from the same source of power. "The rulers of the Gentiles lord it over them. . . . It shall not be so among you; . . . whoever would be great among you must be your servant . . . ; even as the Son of man came not to be served but to serve." (Matt. 20:25-26, 28.)

Man's social hunger, we are told, is as insatiable as physical hunger; he needs friends as badly as he needs food. The sense of belonging, the feeling of rejection; the toxemia of loneliness, the robustness of the socially well-adjusted—we hear a great deal about such matters. And there are those who can help the weak develop social vigor and warn the robust against misdirecting their social energies. Is not this epitomized in the evil proposal that Jesus win social acceptance by a stunt? Imagine the Temple courts filled with people, the sight of a figure high on the glittering dome, paused for a suicidal plunge, the sudden leap, the anguished gasp from the multitude, the graceful landing, the astonishment and relief, and finally the wondering inquiry of the unharmed figure as to who he was and how he did it.

Here again, had this been the story, it would have made a pretty tale. Before then and since there have been prodigious individuals who used their power to ingratiate or dazzle the crowd or by some portent to cajole acceptance. Nor does our censure fall very heavily on them. There is no harm, we say, in winning one's way by superior wit or wisdom or nimbleness; only when acceptance is gained and one's followers abused does it become morally repugnant. Remember Hitler and his ilk.

The power our Lord had for winning acceptance must have fascinated his followers, but he made up his mind in the wilderness that his way with people was not to be won by stunt or subterfuge. To allow angels to bear him up in their hands lest he dash his foot against a stone—this, he said, was to tempt God. Why? Because God had given him power, power to tempt God into allowing him to win people by magic rather than by a way of life. The prospect of his misusing it might tempt God to intercept the consequences of his beloved Son's possible folly, and that would have been to expect of God something he does not do.

3

Again, man's power is exercised in the moral domain. He is so endowed that he can within limits manipulate the physical and social environment to suit his needs and whims. This is impressive power; but the capacity for disturbing the moral order for his advantage is an awesome gift. Gift it indubitably is. Somewhat carelessly, perhaps, we call it freedom and mean little more than that man seems to be able to do as he pleases. This shallow understanding is not to be criticized here. It is necessary only to point out that this sense of power is in the heart of every man. It, more than egotism, is the *fons et origo* of sin. Certainly, then, he who had been called the beloved Son was aware of it. Was he not also precociously sensitive to its abuse?

This is what the third temptation seems to be saying. Again the evil suggestion was not that he really did not have the power by moral artifice to win the world. The apparent willingness of the evil one to sell out his holdings for a price carries the sly intimation that he knew the power of the beloved Son was invincible, and a bargain profitable to himself might be struck. And again we are constrained to observe that if Jesus had accepted the proposition and from that point on held the world firmly in unchallenged possession, there are many of us who might feel the price was not too great to pay for the "kingdoms of the world and the glory of them." What, indeed, would we not give for them? Do not we talk about peace at *any* price?

We must believe that his power to manipulate the moral order was real, else the temptation to do so was fictitious. And that the world was alluring. He wanted it. In describing the experience he recalls the "glory" that was offered for the price of a genuflection. Is not the glory of the world, and by that is meant not tinsel but its solid magnificence, more important than the moral order? And if one has the power—as each of us deeply thinks he has—to purchase solid glory by a momentary compromise, should we not use it? All that was asked of Jesus was a gesture of momentary fealty, not undying loyalty to evil. He had the power to make the gesture but didn't. Worship and service of the Lord God, he replied, are the only allowed uses of one's moral power. This goes pretty deep into the nature of moral obligation.

4

I have been trying to say that the temptations of Jesus sum up his awareness of the power with which he was endowed and the areas within which it was to be exercised. To have moved through this experience with no sense of power would have reduced the whole episode to mirage. The exalted sense of power, separated as it was from all auxiliary supports, makes his proper use of power the greater achievement. This to those who loved him was good news, but we think that it became a part of the gospel because Jesus was identifying his ordeal with that of all men. Each time he replied to the suggestion of the evil one, he did so not in personal terms but in words that within the tradition of Israel included all mankind. *"Man,"* he said, "shall not live by bread alone"; *"you* shall not put the Lord your God to the test" (quoting Deut. 6:16); and, *"You* shall fear the Lord your God; *you* shall serve him and swear by his name" (Deut. 5:13). The wilderness experience makes sense only to those who are aware of their own endowment of power; it has moral value to those who see that the use of power determines the kind of person one is. It is good news, we say, though of such gravity that we do not throw our hats into the air about it.

This filament of man's sense of power and his responsibility for its use is bright in the texture of the Judeo-Christian history. When the new Christian fellowship was organized for sharing the new good news with the world, it was promised not that its members should be shorn of power or reduced to automata but that they would receive power when the Holy Spirit came upon them, and in this new access of strength they would find their way to the uttermost parts of the earth. This was good news, for to the world's impotence there was to be shouted the word that man is uniquely a creature of power. What then is he to do with it? Does the gospel in the Temptations have a suggestion for that?

CHAPTER III

The Integrity of Law

Man's sense of power is unaccompanied by directives. It is not enough to claim or to be assured that one is endowed with simple or with self-conscious power that is to be exercised in the physical, social, and moral orders within which one is set. Lord Acton has been almost wearisomely quoted as having said that power tends to corrupt and absolute power to corrupt absolutely. This has been used as a warning to those who aspire to the places and postures of power. It waggles a finger and says the risk of absolute corruption is a far greater hazard than the modest reward of relative impotence. One might observe that if one ever achieved absolute power, one of its components would be the power of protection against inner tendencies to corruption. Or that the absolute power of God, which is as close as we can come to the idea, should tend to absolute purity instead of absolute corruption. But then, of course, man is not God.

In any case power as it has been discussed here needs a monitor. "Power," says Paul Tillich, "presupposes . . . something over which it proves its power"; and again, "Everybody and everything has chances and must take risks, because his and its power of being remains hidden if actual encounters do not reveal it." [1] The actual encounter of the power of Jesus during his ordeal in the wilderness—and by inference the similar temptations of all men—with "chances" and "risks" brought it, in Tillich's phrase, out of hiding.

His responses to the suggestions of the evil adversary were, as has been said, a refusal to use the physical, social, and

[1] *Love, Power, and Justice* (New York: Oxford University Press, 1954), pp. 37, 41.

moral orders to aggrandize himself or to exhibit his power. But this is not enough, and we are therefore not surprised to discover a positive attitude that paralleled his negative attitude of self-restraint. This may be stated as his determination to preserve the integrity of the physical, social, and moral orders, not only not to misuse but to protect. And again it may be suggested that Jesus, as he identified himself with humanity, was saying in what he did what man also must do to put himself in proper relation to his world. This was part of the good news, inexplicit perhaps but essential to it.

1

Because power inclines to engender loyalty to nothing but itself, it needs a guardrail of loyalty to something external to itself. Oswald Spengler somewhere predicted that the barbaric power that for centuries had been hidden beneath the formal strength of high culture was to reawaken—that warlike sound of joy in one's own power—the will of the strong, the sound instincts to possess and dominate. Recent years have not been without confirmation of this frightening prophecy, and we may be even closer to its fulfillment than some of our pessimists are saying. To those of us who are still able to see in the experiment of Jesus a norm for the successful confrontation of life it is not yet necessary to yield to this dour mood.

It is easy to discern what the positive approach to life was as Jesus faced up to it in the wilderness. Simply put, it was a determination to stay within the orbit of law. It is only a variant of this idea to say he was not going to get outside the will of God. When a man for reasons of pride or avarice or anger decides to take things into his own hands, or to mark out an orbit for his own private gyrations, which is sin, he gets into trouble.

Observe again the proposal to convert a stone into bread.

THE INTEGRITY OF LAW

"If you are the Son of God," whispered the evil voice. But it was precisely because he was God's Son that he could not do it. God has ordained an order in which the ingredients of stone cannot be converted into the ingredients of bread. To assume, then, that one may, for whatever reason, subvert this order is impious. Even the starving Son of God was to be fed only by those foods which the earth in the providence of God provided for him. "Man shall not live by bread alone," said Jesus; and he might have added that he does not live by stone at all. That which is stone is stone; that which is spirit is spirit. But the evil one keeps saying to man, "If you are God's Son, you may with impunity break the law."

This has significance, as we readily see, far beyond the wilderness of temptation. It reaches into the wilderness of all human experience. It is related to the general grounds upon which the still debated subject of miracle may be understood. It is one of the reasons why the whole business of sacramentalism needs to be reconsidered. By what pious legerdemain can an act or thing be imbued with qualities that are not native to its essence? Command this stone to be made bread —thus the sinister voice. Command this bread to be made flesh and this wine, blood—thus the sacramentalist voice. We refuse to accept the former; we consecrate the latter. It should be clear that transubstantiation and some other sacramental practices were ruled out in the first brisk encounter in the wilderness; for we may put it down as axiomatic that life will not allow us—and this is perhaps the most important discipline to which we must conform—to violate the integrity of the physical order. For its violation the inscrutable power and intention of God may make room in our thoughts of him, but it can have no space in our thinking about ourselves. And what a safeguard it is. Suppose we could convert stones into bread by word or toil or into music or

27

poetry or adoration, or virtue—what a chaos we would create. Man, sensing his power, must also sense that over which—to refer to Tillich again—he proves his power. He may test his power and find it meager; or he may flaunt his power and destroy himself, or worse, his cosmos.

2

In the case of Jesus and his approach to man in the aggregate—the Temple court thronging with worshipers in the mood, possibly, for miracle—the issue is hardly so clear for the reason that social laws are less precisely defined than physical laws. This is part of the explanation for sociology's pariah status among the exact sciences. Stones cannot be kneaded into edible loaves, but what are the essences that prevent a miscellany of people becoming a fellowship of devotees? Or how can the refusal of our Lord to leap from the Temple be regarded as anything but another evidence of a disinclination, dictated by prudence as well as by principle, to challenge a physical law, this time the law of gravitation?

Man's first effort at adaptation to life is physical, but very soon the world of social relations begins to invade his tiny world, and sooner or later, since he will have to decide what his fellow creatures are and how he will use them, he finds himself enmeshed in moral complications. Sometimes these are purely moral, sometimes legal. Jesus, we assume, had normal social desires and needs. That they might be satisfied by trickery was proposed, and the proposition was given a sickly cast of piety: God would not let him get hurt in the performance of the stunt. The auspices were good—people at worship in the Temple—the opportunity was ripe for extravaganza; the possibility of reward was plausible.

He declined. The sophistry of the scripture reference to angels intercepting his fall was exposed. He was not going to put God to that sort of proof. But what was the law the integrity of which he was protecting? Recalling the fact that social or psychological laws do not have the standing that laws in the physical sciences have, an answer may be suggested. By first setting forth a fallacy, the principle may, I think, be exposed.

It is generally believed that an extraordinary act means an extraordinary actor. If a man catapults himself from the top of a building without injury, he must be some sort of superman. The fact is he may be a fool. What attracts the crowd is not the person but the trick. Let a cleverer trickster come along, and he steals the show. Thus the high diver, to hold popular following, must jump from a dizzier height each time. There will come a time in the crowd mind when leaping from the temple dome is kid stuff; and if something bigger and more hair-raising is not offered, they will seek livelier amusement elsewhere.

This, I think, is important. The Romans, to entertain the restless populace, started with bread and circuses and ended throwing Christians to the lions. When clowns got tiresome, gladiators were brought to the arena. This neither won loyalty to Rome nor gave the emperor the satisfaction of having contented people.

The mistake is made in thinking that magic makes the magician, when the reverse is true. Therefore if people in the aggregate are to be won and held for something worthy of their dignity as sons of God, something more important than bigger and better supercolossal shows must be offered them. It must be a bigger and better man, or idea. This is not easy for us in an entertainment-glutted society to believe. Kant came as close to putting it in the form of a law as we shall get it: treat man never simply as a means but always at the same time as an end. For Kant immoral actions issued only from that which contradicted the true nature of man. Judged by this criterion the leap from the Temple top would have been an exploitation, not a contradiction, of a powerful human impulse—the love of the spectacular—for Jesus' own advantage. It does not alter the case to say that to be his followers was the best thing that could possibly have happened to the people. Had he won them by a trick, they would hardly have died for a faith. When he invited Peter and Andrew to "come and see," they did not follow him to a sorcerer's cave.

The Christian Church needs to remember this. So also must our democratic society. There must be more than pulpit sensationalism in the one and political spoofing in the other, but to say this is to moralize. Let it suffice to note that in a way more profound than the world is generally willing to concede, Jesus saw a law of social and psychological importance that he could not break. He was often to enter the Temple in later days and once to drive its exploiters out. This he could do because he had kept faith with what he believed man to be. If we could keep that faith—but that's moralizing again.

This belongs with the gospel for the reason that it is good news. It is idle to speculate what would have happened if Jesus had either flattered or browbeaten the people. Some world shakers have won brief following by regarding the mob as a beast and whipping it. Tyrants do have a way with them, and man has his servile impulses as surely as he has the fever of revolt in his soul. Others have played paterfamilias to the crowds and held them by promise and pampering. Patronage does have something to say for it, and man loves to be fondled as truly as he loves to fight. But these are the ways of the exploiters who use the mob in the Temple or market place for their own ends. To regard each member of the multitude as being above the indignity of solicitation by trickery is unthinkable for them. For this reason we find in this familiar episode something that the Christian testimony has always held in its heart although its advocates have not always held it in their hands; and that Jesus saw value so great, even in men in the mass, that he would not traduce their worth by a cheap trick is something we must not allow ourselves to forget.

3

This brings us to the third episode. Social laws are imprecise; and since moral law is to a degree the funded experience of society, it follows that it also may have blunt edges. Studies recently conducted in an eastern university would seem to have established the fact that in all cultures there is a rudimentary moral consensus. This is to be expressed in principle rather than code; for example, it is always right to do right, always wrong to do wrong. This may sound like a platitude when in fact it is the base of all morality. If it were anywhere regarded as right to do what was recognized as wrong, there would moral chaos be found.

In our own culture there is one pillar on which our moral structure rests; the inviolable dignity of the individual. This is supported by two giant buttresses; might does not make right; the end does not justify the means. A good deal of the moral confusion of our times lies in the fact that we seem to be trying to support the first by denying the second. We are guilty of using means for protecting man against morality-by-might that end up in denying the dignity and destroying the culture of those who dispute our moral norms.

Now it would seem that in the third temptation Jesus was struggling with these three great ethical principles each of which was, we assume, denied by the adversary. A cynical contempt for human dignity is, we say, demonic or just plain devilish; conformity to code—no matter what sort—by coercion is no less satanic; and the use of evil means to secure righteous ends is, we grandly say, the essence of diabolism. Was Jesus to preserve the integrity of the moral law? Was he to employ an evil means to achieve a lofty end? We know the answer, of course; but that he was tempted to make a trade, we must believe lest the whole report he gave be chimerical.

Luke's record embellishes the simple report with the claim of the evil one that the kingdoms of the world and all their power and splendor (4:6-7) had been handed over to him and that he could convey title to whomsoever he wished. Since the devil has rarely been modest in his claims, we may assume that he included in his inventory the peoples of the world, who added and gave meaning to the power and splendor of this vision. All this was his, he said, and could be held forever in fee simple by anyone on whom his favor rested. That is, for a price, of course.

The price was a gesture of allegiance. This was surely history's greatest bargain day. To which the prospective buyer said, "Begone, Satan! for it is written, 'You shall worship the Lord your God, and him only shall you serve'" (Matt. 4:10).

The moral law, the integrity of which Jesus was protecting, was that man is not to be bought and sold, and that even so seemingly slight a gesture of compromise was not to be allowed no matter if the reward was to be the possession of the world and its teeming peoples. There are perhaps those who agree that Satan was right in his claim to possession of the world, though who handed it over to him and why poses a question or two. We have no record of Jesus' reaction to this boast. Had he agreed, he would have been faced with the problem of what end God had in mind and why he had used the devil as an accomplice. This is the problem that haunts those who agree, at least, that man through divine connivance is evil, that he has a congenital black drop in his blood that he inherited from his hapless ancestors in

Eden, and that he can purge it only by the grace of him who by complicity or allowance injected it into his veins. This is the contradiction that confuses the doctrine of original sin; it pits God's primary error against his ultimate grace.

It is my contention that in Jesus' act, as he reported his spiritual wrestling, the devil's ownership was repudiated; and an evil way of possessing for himself the world he was to redeem (by posturing in devotion before evil) was similarly repudiated. If he was to possess the world, it was to be by worship and service to God, and not by a conciliatory nod in the direction of the adversary.

4

Thus we see our Lord, conscious of power, refusing to employ it for his own advantage and using it to protect the integrity of law in the area of physical, social, and moral experience. Why did he tell this story, and why was it made a part of the evangel? If not for vainglory then it would seem to have been because to mankind as well as to himself the conflict and its issue were good news. Man is endowed with power—that is the meaning of conflict—and he can use his power to preserve the integrity of the order God has established—that is the meaning of victory.

This is not the whole story; it is, as Mark puts it, the beginning of the gospel of Jesus Christ the Son of God. It was a good beginning. Jesus in an isolation as awesome as it was complete, separated from human and divine auxiliaries, confronted life and won. After his victory, as the story has it, angels came and ministered to him. Why had they not come along when he was flanked by the ingratiating voices of disobedience, pride, and compromise? This we cannot confidently answer, but there may be a suggestion of importance in the circumstance. In this struggle he stood alone as the Son of man rather than as the Son of God. No advantage was his that was not man's. It was the devil who taunted him with the title Son of God; when Jesus answered, he included himself in the generic "you."

We cannot press this analysis too far. It is enough to say again—and it must be said often—that Jesus, confronting life and dramatizing the experience in the profound parable of the Temptations, affirmed something about man that is basic to the biblical understanding of man's nature. It was not something that bubbled up in sentimentality; it was something that was wrought out in struggle. It is not mock heroics to say we must struggle much as he did and with less prospect of victory because life is more formidable and evil more ruthless and cynical. Nor is it shoddy optimism to say that man can stand up to life with a measure of self-confidence that is not sinful pride. "It is the way the Master went," says a familiar hymn and asks, "Should not the servant tread it still?" Here is a ground of hope that need not withdraw into eschatology. Indeed, it may—and will—often withdraw into the wilderness alone, not to go down whimpering in defeat but to emerge in the company of angels.

CHAPTER IV

Salt, Light, and Beatitude

"You are the salt of the earth. . . . You are the light of the world." (Matt. 5:13, 14.) This is a handsome compliment. To whom was it addressed?

The readiest answer is that Jesus was speaking to his disciples only. He had seen the crowds, gone up the mountain, and sat down. When his disciples came to him, he opened his mouth and taught *them*. What we call the Beatitudes follow, nine states of mind or circumstance that are productive of the sense of well-being. "Euphoria" is the currently popular synonym for Matthew's "blessed" (*makarioi*).

There is support for this limited application of these gay reassurances. The chances are that the group had been together long enough and had already been sufficiently aggressive to have encountered resistance and odium. If this was their reward for announcing the good news that the kingdom of heaven after centuries of delay was now at hand, they needed a tonic. It was necessary to tell men whose early enthusiasm might have lost its savor and whose bright confidence had been overcast by disappointment that they were both salt and light and that their discouragements could be understood as blessedness. Such persons were just what the jaded and gloomy times needed.

There are other groups identified as the targets of these words, they were intended as mandatory only for those who were already in the kingdom or for those who soon would be, or as interim guidance for those who were and are waiting for the kingdom's coming, or for those who post mortem are to live forever in the Elysium of the blessed. The reason for such divergence of opinion arises largely from the fact that in the practical world of human affairs the Sermon on the Mount seems either impossible or impractical or imprudent or even plain foolishness. We are unable to jack ourselves up high enough to see it as shot menacingly at us. Therefore we tend to hide or to deflect it toward others who can better stand its puncturing volleys.

Here is undertaken no reconciliation of these honest scholarly differences. What I do want to say is that his words reflect an attitude Jesus had respecting men, in general and in particular, that is not measurably affected by the various identifications of his audience. This is to be seen by simply exchanging the benedictions of Matt. 5 for the maledictions of Matt. 23. Instead of "blessed" read "woe"; woe unto you, insipid; woe unto you, smoldering wicks; wretched you who hunger and thirst, who mourn and who suffer persecution. Or, blessed, you scribes and Pharisees, hypocrites who tithe mint, anise, and cummin and neglect the weightier matters of the law; or blessed are you blind fools who think that the gift is greater than the altar (Matt. 23:18). Such a transfer reduces any ethical maxims to absurdity. It was the hypocrisy, the deliberate masquerade, of the Pharisees that excited our Lord's rebuke; similarly it was some deep and perhaps unconscious resource to which he was appealing in his confident guarantee of blessedness. This resource the Pharisee and the disciple alike possessed.

Jesus, as has been pointed out before, gave the impression that "he knew all men and needed no one to bear witness of man; for he himself knew what was in man" (John 2:25). This may be taken to mean that he held to what we call a doctrine of man though nowhere is it explicitly set forth. It is to be found, therefore, by deduction, something that in this case is fairly simple since all he taught was predicated on what he thought man's resources for understanding him were.[1] Here in the perspective within which he saw human nature are nothing of sentimentality, nothing of condescension, and nothing of misanthropy. Because he knew men, he loved and encouraged them; because he knew men, he warned and rebuked them. For this reason we hesitate almost as much to call him an optimist as a pessimist. It is enough to appropriate the appraising words of John: "he knew."

1

So when he said, "You are the salt. . . . You are the light," he was, we are assured, saying something about human nature. He promptly made allowance for the dilution of salt—the only way salt loses its savor. Mix a cup of sand and a cup of salt, and the result is insipid. Shopkeepers have apparently used this trick since salt was first offered for sale. He made allowance also for the diminution of light by hiding it under a basket or a bed. But salt, the quality that enhances the savor of the food it is used on, and light, the quality that casts illumination and fructifies growth—these are both basic and unique in the human personality. How else is mortal life to have zest, how else be irradiated and activated from inertia to action?

We can agree that Jesus may have felt his little circle of friends to have relatively more highly developed qualities of salt and light, and surely we like to think that those of us within the fellowship of the kingdom have more zest and sparkle than those who are outside. But can we honestly believe that *only* we are salt and light? This is inadmissible in the light (salt) of what is found in cultures different from

[1] Brunner and the biblical theology school in general would object to this on the grounds that we seem to assume human intelligence and responsibility sufficient for an understanding of God's demands. Exactly; for while Jesus was often misunderstood, it reflects slight credit on him to say that he talked over his hearers' heads or deliberately taunted them with impossible proposals.

our own. Salt is diluted and trodden under the feet of men, and light is derided and mischievously snuffed out; but if it were not true that every man born into the world brings with him his own mysterious endowment of zest and the capacity to glow, cultures would die. More accurately, perhaps, culture would never come to be. This fact irrespective of its relation to Jesus' ideas is part of the ground of optimism on which faith in God must rest. There is in man a candle that may be kindled into brilliance, a taste that may be cultivated into charm. To do this is one way of regarding the purpose of redemption; that such may become the sons of God. We must take care lest the inspidity and shadow of much of life constrain us to deny that there is despite it all salt and light in each of us. We are salt and light: that's good news.

2

I have commented on the salt and light metaphors because they are, together with the city on a hill that cannot be hid (a social extension of the personal endowment of salt and light), a sort of quick summary of the Beatitudes. What this means, it is necessary to state in more particular terms.

A look at the Beatitudes shows that they are divisible into three groups. The first deals with those dark experiences of life that have their center within the spirit of the man. They are familiar as poverty of spirit, mourning, and a hunger and thirst for righteousness. The second group deals with the bright experiences of life. They also have their center within the spirit: meekness, mercy, purity, and peacemaking. The third group deals with dark experiences again, but this time they are caused by aggression from the outside: persecution for righteousness' sake and reviling, persecution and false accusation on Jesus' account. In all these cases there is a promise of reward which is part of the blessedness.

Now the point here is that Jesus said these things because "he knew what was in man." Did he assume that there was an emotional resiliency that could be counted on to enable man to weather life's rough waters, to survive the dark turbulence into which he is inescapably led? Or was Jesus commited to the notion that life is too formidable a contest for man, that he is foredoomed by the nature of his own spirit to fall before life's merciless pummeling? Had the latter been his faith—or fatalism—to have spoken as he did to those in distress would have been dishonest. To promise them blessedness here and now (in only one case did he say the reward would be great in heaven) would have seemed to them either blindness or insensitivity. After all, what blessing is there in persecution unless in man's soul there is something that can transcend and transmute it? Otherwise it were better to say outright that life is a tough adversary and you can't win, because not only does man not have what it takes; he is foredoomed by a spiritual sickness that he has inherited.

When then are the poor in spirit? Not the corrupt but the spent, the weary, the dismayed, the torpid. There is ground for rendering *ptochos* also "lowly or depressed." Indeed, the poor in spirit are all of us at one time or another. And when our resistance threshold is lowered by fatigue or spiritual penury, and we cannot keep out the invasion of ponderous or even petty irritations, we protest against life and blame our depression on everything except the real cause of it. Oddly enough there is true blessedness in this shadowed mood because it exhibits that the spirit of man is a living thing, sensitive to the cycles of gaiety and gloom that are as normal as fatigue and replenishment. What a sorry thing living would be if it were all sunshine. If blessedness is the private possession only of the happy, it can have no solid meaning.

What has been said about depletion of spirit is given

further point by the blessing promised the sorrowing. Here again there is no blessing in mourning per se. To think so would make melancholy the pathway to happiness. There are too many people who think that to be really happy they must be sad and adduce this word of Jesus to support their neurotic whining. Sorrow is not the nature of the spirit of man though the capacity for tears is a valuable human asset. Mourning is one of the dark experiences through which he is able to pass because he has inner resources that make the passage possible.

Again, hunger and thirst for righteousness are to be similarly understood. Here is one of man's finest endowments, if indeed not his finest. It is the response of the spirit to rightness, to what is better than average and fairer than ordinary. It is these spiritually insatiable who are satisfied, not in terms of getting hold at last of the ultimate in goodness, beauty, and truth, but in the ever-increasing advance of the spirit toward the never-attainable satisfactions of perfection. These are not those who stop, assess their hunger and thirst, and lament that somehow they cannot assimilate food or water because their basal spiritual metabolism is congenitally inadequate to furnish sufficient energy to keep them spiritually alive. Man, this seems to say, has a hunger for righteousness, not a revulsion toward it; and this yearning is of itself a blessing. Suppose innately man had only a hunger for evil, that all his basic impulses and drives were sinister and sinful. Some have come very close to saying this, and the condition they describe is hardly to be classified as beatitude.

3

What is to be said of the second group, which deals with life's bright experiences? We should have no trouble here, for it flatters us to think that we may be thought meek, merciful, pure in heart, and the makers of peace, even though we admit that for any number of reasons we do not cultivate these states very assiduously.

Meek: Gerald Heard argues cogently that the word carries the meaning of discipline.

The Greek testament word . . . is *praos*. For what did Greeks use it? They used it for wild animals which had been tamed, trained, for wild horses which had been made able to work with men. There is then in this definition, nothing weak or spiritless but rather the description of an energy which, instead of exploding, is now channeled and directed.[2]

A French rendering of this Beatitude puts it: *Hereux les debonnaires, car ils heriteront de la terre.* Debonair is a gay synonym for meekness; but whether we prefer discipline or lightness of heart, the suggestion that the meek are not necessarily foot mats or jellyfish is reassuring.

Here again we have a suggestion of what Jesus knew about man. The disciplined *do* inherit the earth, but they are the self-disciplined. And what greater blessing can be pronounced than that man *can* discipline himself? Not wholly nor always, but neither is he confined to a spiritual strait jacket nor condemned to run wild and unbridled and thus destroy himself. He who is serious about bridling his tongue (Jas. 1:26) will trust neither to his own strength nor to criteria he has improvised for the moment, but the effort will be his own.

Mercy: here is a mighty word. It can carry on its back almost the whole weight of Christian obligation. Its lineage is ancient: man's duty to Jehovah was partly discharged by loving mercy (Mic. 6:8), and today what better than compassion can be put forth as the essence of the Christian spirit? Does man have the impulse to be merciful? Is compassion a mood alien to the spirit of man? If he is let alone in the presence

---

[2] *The Code of Christ* (New York: Harper & Bros., 1941), pp. 63-64.

of suffering, will his inclinations move him toward pity or cruelty? There is something that will break through the barriers of organized and disciplined enmity to offer a cup of cold water in the name of mercy. If indeed this is not a component of the human spirit, however neglected it may be, then we must find something deceivingly like it to account for much that goes on in cultures of the world.

The pure in heart: we speak softly here knowing the easy corruptions of our own spirits. Are there any who are pure in heart, a condition that may be proved by their vision of God? If saint is not a pseudonym for pious humbug, there are those described by Emerson as "jubilant and beholding souls" who are known to us. We do not need to name them; they will rarely name themselves, for they have achieved their status not by accolade but by action. Theirs is the ultimate Beatitude, for they have been able to see God both high and lifted up evoking their devotion, and crying with the voice of human wretchedness begging an alms (Matt. 25: 31-46). It is important to realize that Jesus was saying this about mortal men. However restricted his audience may have been or however colored his words by a fancied *eschatos*, he was not talking about angels or demigods. If a man did not have something within him that was at least as amenable to purification as to corruption, to talk about the "pure in heart" would have been frivolous. To see God may not be the proof of saintliness, but the saint will see him. Jesus was hardly talking to or about the utterly pure. The saint, like salt, may lose his savor; but unlike salt, the saint can recover it.

There remains the matter of peacemaking, that enterprise of men that wins them the title sons of God. In the making of peace and winning the happy name man does not become any less a son of man. The peacemaker accepts no new status. We have perhaps thought too little as to what this involves.

After all, in human relations can peace be made by any effort except man's? This eliminates nothing of the divine grace that is both the impetus and the support of the peacemaker. But God has already given us the resources out of which peace can be fashioned. We do him little honor when we pray that he send peace on the earth. He has entrusted the "message of reconciliation" (II Cor. 5:19) to us, not to seraphs in the shining sky. To be sure, man's aptitude for conflict seems more highly specialized in our times, and that is his sin; but the mandate to make peace has not been withdrawn for the reason that there is nowhere else that it can be laid. Man as a peacemaker often seems to us a shiftless and impotent spectacle, but he who knew what is in man said he had the power to perform the magic of God's sons as well as the sorcery of the sons of hell. The one should make us proud as the other makes us ashamed.

4

There are two kinds of persecution promised those who heard this teacher who knew what was in man. The first was persecution for righteousness' sake; the second was for false indictment. In general, persecution is the undeserved abuse suffered by good people; punishment is the merited recompense of bad behavior. Or persecution is the penalty of goodness. This latter might be construed as a somewhat cynical judgment concerning moral cause and effect. We do not think that things are so topsy-turvy as that. But Jesus seems to have been considering a moral imbalance that has been apparent to all sensitive spirits. It was once stated thus:

> Think now, who that was innocent ever perished?
> Or where were the upright cut off? (Job 4:7.)

This was the jaunty optimism of Eliphaz. But Job's pessimism was just as distorted:

> I shall be condemned;
> why then do I labor in vain?
> If I wash myself with snow,
> and cleanse my hands with lye,
> yet thou wilt plunge me into a pit
> and my own clothes will abhor me. (9:29-31.)

The punishment of evil offers us no difficulty; it is the persecution of the good that troubles us. Morally it seems to indicate blindness or indifference somewhere. Job says despairingly:

> There is no umpire between us
> who might lay his hand upon us both. (9:33.)

But practically speaking the question persists: If a man is persecuted for being good and punished for being bad, what is the difference and what is he to do? "Rejoice and be glad," said Jesus. For two reasons: your reward will be great in heaven, and you will stand in the thin red line of the prophets who suffered the same injustice and humiliation. Neither of these reasons is likely to be convincing to those who have found that their efforts at being good won them not only maleficence but an inner sense of injustice. Unless we can find in what Jesus said something that rests on a level deeper than that of simple moral cause and effect, we must decline the Beatitude.

This is found, I think, not on the level of action but on the level of man's essential nature. Here again we are brought back to the statement that Jesus knew what was in man. In the exhortation to regard persecution as blessed he was dealing not so much with external factors as with man's inner resources for meeting them. Man's desire and capacity for righteousness are so considerable that they need not give way before indifference or hostility. In other words righteousness that lasts only so long as it is applauded is not righteousness at all; it is opportunism. It is exactly this that Jesus was talking about when he demanded that righteousness must exceed the "righteousness" of the scribes and Pharisees. Somehow we have never thought of Pharisees being persecuted for their righteousness, though when they felt the whiplash of the Master's tongue against their thin-skinned hypocrisy, they no doubt thought they were suffering for their cultivated skill in the formal rituals of piety. At the same time they must have known that they were not in line with the prophets who were before them. They, said Jesus, were "sons of those who murdered the prophets."

5

This will perhaps not make us much less disinclined to shun persecution for righteousness' sake. To be persecuted is to be at odds with one's fellows, and to be socially *en rapport* has come close to furnishing the code of righteousness to which we aspire. So we will rejoice at flattery and recoil from rebuke, and pride will seem a safer monitor than persecution and self-pity. All of which is simply to say that the problem is not solved on the superficial levels of life by repeating a Beatitude that has been identified by some as a weak defense of one's neurotic satisfaction in being abused. It was, we may believe, another evidence of what Jesus saw in man: the innate possibility of a rightness that was invincible even against assault by those who leveled their barrage in the name of their own righteousness. It was a *capacity* to which Jesus referred, a capacity which, as almost nothing else in the human spirit, can be truly called blessing.

6

In sum, then, it has been said that the Beatitudes provide for us a window into the mind of Jesus. "He knew what was in man," and we believe we can see something of what was in him. Unless we are prepared to dismiss his gay-hearted reassurances as sentimentality, we must accept them as a matured confidence in the stuff of man's soul. Beneath the dark experiences of spiritual depletion, grief, and moral insufficiency there was the capacity for refreshment, joy, and satisfaction. Beneath the bright levels of compassionateness, self-discipline, purity, and pacification was the native endowment of soul from which these impulses take rise. And beneath the bewildering disorder of reward and penalty, persecution and punishment, and the vehemence of "righteousness" against righteousness there was that superlative inner something that could so truly mount above and change it that the heart could be heard singing above the din because it was exceeding glad.

We need to be reminded at this point that what Jesus thought about man might have been mistaken, wholly or in part. The studies of countless students have tested his insights. So he has been called dreamer, fanatic, and fool. And correlatively, man has been called fallen angel, dupe, and beast. This argument will not soon be adjourned. For the present and as long as we may, we shall take such modest satisfactions as we can in the fact that when Jesus first confronted the people he came to save from their sins, his opening word, as Matthew gives it, was "blessed."

CHAPTER V

Fulfillment of the Law

It is difficult to see how Jesus could have undertaken so important a mission as fulfilling law and prophecy if he did not accept the basis on which they had so long rested. The ground on which the funded experience of his people —which was the law—and the immediate, contemporary, and regulating voice of God—which was prophecy—this ground was, I believe, an optimistic view of the nature of man. Not the naïve optimism or the amiable liberalism with which such a view is sometimes slandered, but an optimism that began in the sense that man was created in the divine image and was covenanted to God in a purpose that was not to be diverted and a power that was not to be debilitated. Such a notion was sorely tried; indeed, the history of our Lord's people is largely the record of man's conflict with his Creator, a conflict through which he was gradually to grow in understanding and self-control.

Defection and return, sin and forgiveness, worship in the groves of Astarte and sacrifice before the altar of the Eternal; haughtiness and self-reproach, wisdom and stupidity, life and death—thus the record puts it. God is represented as repenting the folly of creation, consumed with vengeful anger against man's faithlessness, and yet, conversely, "slow to anger, and plenteous in mercy" (K.J.V.).

Nevertheless God in the law assumed man's capacity to obey the law as well as to flout it, and in the prophets he spoke to him words of compassion as well as judgment. Nowhere, however, did he quit, though some of his spokesmen report him as getting pretty close to it. Was it because his stake in man was too great to abandon?

> He leads me in paths of righteousness
> for his name's sake,

said the poet. Not for man's sake, primarily, or to protect the good name of his earth progeny but for *his own name's sake,* to preserve his own reputation. This would seem to have been a confidence on the Creator's part that was too sturdy to be called naïve. Perhaps it is because we who have less confidence in God and less to lose in man dismiss him as "irremediably corrupt," as one contemporary theologian has put it.

In any case Jesus, who was fulfilling the law and the prophets, did not go about the job by destroying them or the base on which they seemed—sometimes precariously—to rest. So we are not surprised to hear him encouraging those to whom he had propounded the Beatitudes to let their light shine and their good works be seen in order that the Father in heaven might have his stake in humanity protected. Such display, Jesus cautioned, must not be the pretentious Pharisaic righteousness which was not so much an expression of the inner spirit as the counterfeit currency with which popular applause was bought. "Not an iota, not a dot, will pass from the law until all is accomplished," he said. We assume that the accomplishing was to be understood in terms of the fulfillment of the divine purposes for mankind. The aid of law and prophecy in this cosmic redemption was not to be discarded. And that would seem to imply that the idea of the nature of man on which law and prophecy were predicated was no less impregnable.

1

Fulfillment, I think, meant extension rather than contraction of man's resources for righteousness and his understanding of his moral responsibilities. Man is maddeningly perverse in his refusal or disinclination or incapacity for sharpening the edge of his ethical sensitiveness, but this does not provide us an accurate or final gauge of his spirit. I say this because in the explicit instructions that follow the Beatitudes Jesus is clearly making the effort to whet the law and the prophets to keener sharpness. On the contrary, had he lost his confidence in man's capacities for an improved quality of righteousness, he would most certainly have taken a different approach. Thus he could have said: "You have heard that it was said to the men of old, 'You shall not kill.' But I say to you that the impulse to kill is necessary to survival. It should therefore be cultivated and indulged." This is not so fantastic as it sounds. A widely distributed anonymous pamphlet titled *Pax Americana—The Elite Whiteman's Guidebook* says: "Are we not all predatory animals by instinct? . . . Hate your enemies with a whole heart, and if a man smite you on the cheek, smash him down, smite him hip and thigh, for self-preservation is the highest law," etc. The subcaption of this angry and not implausible document is in the form of a syllogism: Life is struggle; struggle is war; war is life.

When Jesus approached the problem of killing, he sought to appeal neither to the law which forbade it nor to prophecy which sometimes condoned it, but to something deep in the heart of the man who committed it: man's capacity for anger. In Matt. 5:21-22 this implosive energy appears in three ways: simple anger that incurs judgment; insult that invites council action in judgment; and contempt—"You fool!"—that is threatened by consignment to the flames of Gehenna.

It is not important for this study to analyze this inner agitation that is pretty generally considered to be one of the basic human emotions, fear and sex being the other two. But there are three things that may be said about it. The first, if we want to be literalistic, is that when man was created in the image of God, the capacity for anger was kneaded into the dynamic dust. Man may be Godlike in his fury; without it he would be less than man. The Bible is replete with references to the anger of God. It is slow kindling, but it can become a destroying flame. There are times, to be sure, when the devastations of human anger and what we think is the anger of God make us wish that it could be dissolved into serenity, since it is difficult to imagine that the consequences of calm could be as damaging as tempest.

The second observation about anger is that it is not to be dealt with by neutralization or even by undiscriminating suppression. It is not evil; to be born with no capacity for those creative forms that anger can take would result in moral idiocy. This is true despite the moral idiocy that undisciplined anger manifests. No anger: no Moses, no Micah, no Jesus, no Luther—we can also say no God.

If we are to follow the suggestion of our Lord, the third fact about anger is that it can be deflected from destructive manifestations into edifying results. This is what seems to be the point (Matt. 5:23-24) of the abrupt transfer of interest from the angry, insulting, and contemptuous man to the same man on the way to deliver his gift at the altar and the admonition to catch "quickly" this volatile impulse and make it an agent of reconciliation.

How, we ask, does anger thus change its spots? Has not the worshiper simply quieted his stormy temper? As he goes to worship, has not his spirit simply been cleansed of hostility, insult, and contempt? Apparently not, for it is precisely against that that Jesus' warning was directed. Taking one's hostilities to church not only makes meaningless the rituals of devotion; it may give the magistrate time to serve the summons of one's accuser.

2

It is at this point that we begin to see the profound depths to which Jesus looked in seeing what was in man. The angry man with his votive gift is not to go and pray that his ill humor shall be purged; he is to direct his anger at himself. It is his misdirected anger that has estranged him from his fellow and made worship of God a mockery. A tithe of this anger focused at himself for his folly or haste would create a situation productive of happiness all the way 'round. In our experience we must confess that anger rarely seems to do this, but our instructors in the strange behavior of the human spirit have told us that more often than not the things that anger us are not what we think they are, and that if we were able to point our hostility momentarily against ourselves, anger would abate and the whole relation would be seen in clearer light. This does not mean abject, neurotic, introverted guilt feelings. Nothing suggestive of that is found in Jesus' words. And if it were actually practiced—this indignation directed at ourselves—the business of killing would be taken care of as well as the less grievous and more common sins of rudeness and scorn. Jesus was not pessimistic about man's anger nor about its appalling results when misdirected or undisciplined. Anger was part of God's gift to man; it was to be not withdrawn but creatively used.

It is next to impossible to apprehend this wisdom in a world so largely committed to its opposite. Killing, we agree, is the bitter fruit of anger. We have little patience with the sophistry that talks of killing the adversary dispassionately or even in love. No anger, no killing—this is clear. To say, however, that anger at another when directed toward one's self deflects this powerful emotion away from destruction and gives impetus to self-growth, this is so fantastic that to say it makes us furious! So we feel relieved to learn that some scholarly surmising may ease the pressure by saying the Sermon on the Mount was a moral syllabus for saints who were not long for this world. This comes close to taking away the good news for sinners by making it, ironically, applicable only to saints. Nevertheless two deductions are inescapable: first, that he who knew what was in man was not cast into gloom over man's nature even though it included highly inflammable properties. He even obliquely paid man the compliment of saying that this very quality that is the despair of many may also be their hope. The second is that within the ethical cultures of the world we are aware of nothing comparable to Jesus' constructive treatment of this volatile source of so much of the world's long bitterness and death.

3

In this connection a further amplification that is found in 5:38-48 deserves our attention. The consequences of anger are rarely considered as the operation of justice. Passion makes the judge a partisan. When justice—the proportionate distribution of reward and penalty—enters into a conflict situation, the assumption is that anger has been sealed off in order to allow a judicious balancing of all the factors involved.

Hence the ancient maxim of eye for eye and tooth for tooth. The full quotation from Exod. 21:23-25 spells it out more fully: "If any harm follows, then you shall give life for life, eye for eye, tooth for tooth, hand for hand, foot for foot, burn for burn, wound for wound, stripe for stripe." This, of course, falls far short of a complete list since such completeness is impossible. Moreover, in the nature of the case the effort at justice is sure to fall short of satisfaction when thus pursued. No judge can correctly equate one life with another, one eye with another, one wound with another. Accurate exchange is impossible since the blow one suffered might on another's back be little more than a stout caress. The reason is that physical suffering involves psychic trauma that is perhaps its most important aspect. To show the absurdity to which such attempts at justice can lead, one only needs to note the price tag the lovelorn put on their feelings when the judge of the domestic-relations court is asked to adjudicate a fair settlement of their losses.

Jesus, facing both the logic and the results of such justice, introduces the factor of generosity. This, unhappily, goes by the name of appeasement in our times and is regarded as the uttermost obliquity of diplomats in a jam. Thus the scales are thrown away, and abstract justice takes a licking at the hands of sentimental generosity. Cheek for cheek requires of the aggressed a monumental self-control few can muster, though those who have (Gandhi, for example) have measured its phenomenal power. The cloak added to the litigious coat, the extra mile, the gift to the beggar and the loan to the borrower, these are all expressions of a largeness of heart that goes beyond the rigors of justice and are calculated not only to settle an issue but to create a bond. Justice divides, love unites, and it is the latter that creates the fellowship that is the final cancelation of enmity.

This was very important to him who knew what was in man. For this reason there is further reference to it. Anger directed to one's self protects one from aggression toward another; justice converted into generosity creates fellowship. This may sound strange to modern ears, but to those who have ears to hear he has more to say. "You have heard it was said, 'You shall love your neighbor and hate your enemy.' But I say to you, Love your enemies and pray for those who persecute you." (Matt. 5:43-44.)

It is interesting to discover that the author of the First Gospel put on the lips of Jesus words that we do not find in the Law. The neighbor in the ancient codes was to be treated with singular consideration that reached its highest expression in: "Love your neighbor as yourself." But the correlative admonition to hate one's enemy is not a part of the code. How this discrepancy occurred is largely a matter of literary interest. It does not seem fair to the ancients. Perhaps by the time the Gospel was written, the centuries of enmity had crystallized into an established and unwritten code. By that time it seemed plausible, did it not, that if one loved one's neighbor, he would naturally hate his enemy? We have had sufficient experience in the growth of moral attitudes to understand this.

However this puzzle may be resolved by critics, Jesus' use of it is both clear and familiar. He advocates love and prayer as the methods of handling those who, although they are not neighbors, should be treated as such. To direct hostility toward one's self and to be more concerned with generosity than arbitrary justice, hard as they may be in our practical world, are easy as compared with loving and praying for the aggressor. "Hate your enemies with a whole heart," advised the pamphlet quoted above.

The basic difficulty with hate is that it is blinding. Martin Buber says: "Hate is by nature blind. Only a part of a being can be hated. He who sees a whole being and is compelled to reject it is no longer in the kingdom of hate, but is in that of human restriction of the power to say *Thou*." [1] It was, we may assume, Jesus' ability to know what was in man, not by clairvoyance but by discernment, that made it impossible for him to hate even those who were determined to destroy him. He could say *Thou* to every man. And as we have previously observed, his identification of himself with humanity led him to seek for his fellows the same sort of

---

[1] *I and Thou*, tr., R. G. Smith (New York: Chas. Scribner's Sons, 1937), p. 16.

clarity of understanding that had spared him the folly and futility of hate.

Romantic love, for opposite reasons, shares hate's blindness; but it was not this delightful disability that our Lord advocated for our enemy ailments. Agape—aggressive and creative good will—was what he was talking about. This is open-eyed and unblinkered; it can see possibilities hidden behind actualities that neither fright nor failure will black out. Once these are seen, one can pray discerningly for one's persecutor. To pray in hate—and it is not uncommon; What is more terrible, for example, than the prayer "God damn you"?—to pray in hate is to pray blindly, which is no better than not praying at all.

All of this, even going back to his treatment of the destructive and constructive uses of anger, is in the mind of Jesus a practical matter. It is to be followed not by some post-mortem reward but by a new status as sons of the heavenly Father whose justice and generosity are impartially distributed toward the good and evil. To this is added a new and widening fellowship with such strange (And therefore "hateful"?) creatures as tax gatherers and Gentiles; and to crown it all, love of one's enemies confers participation in the divine perfection. Here, of course, the "heavenly Father is perfect" is not to be understood as a statement of metaphysical perfection. So far as man can *know* the perfection of God, it is through his experience of God's generosity and love toward those of us who are, not by nature but by perversity or shortsightedness, often enemies of his. It is of immense importance for us to recover the faith in humanity that Jesus, who knew man more profoundly than we, had. He said that there are some things man can do because he is endowed with the capacity for doing them; and because he can, he must. This can lift him to the level of sharing the perfection of God. For us to say this in the face of man's degradation is to sound insufferably proud. Was he mistaken? Did he see more shallowly than we man's capacities for evil? Was he shouting in the dark when he urged that man let his light shine? Perhaps our inescapable preoccupation with man's sin has made us lose confidence in the light that is in his soul that enables him, if he will, to say *Thou* to everyman.

4

These matters that have engaged us have to do with the problem of getting on with unpleasant people. They run all the way from those who anger us to the point of wanting to kill them to those who annoy us by begging and borrowing. We are not fated to be victimized by them or to defend ourselves by destroying them. Inner resources that are native to man can be employed to transform them—and us—into neighbors we can accept or friends we can love. This is what Jesus said; to believe it requires energetic faith, and to practice it demands prodigies of self-control. Plus, to be sure, the ready resources of the grace and power of God.

It so happens, however, that we are tested morally not only by our enemies but also by our friends. It is not surprising then to find that Jesus took account of this in man and had something to say about it in two particulars. One deals with adultery, the other with taking oaths.

It is precisely because adultery is, so to speak, an affair between friends that its moral aspect is easily played down. Clandestine, it has not the public and dramatic visibility of an angry quarrel or a beggar's nakedness; as an agreement it claims it is the business of nobody else. The eye that rests with satisfaction on the beauty of another and converts wholesome delight into lust is the first aide to sexual sin. The hand that thrills the body with its touch and warms desire with its esurient caress is the second aide. Hand and eye must go, said Jesus. But nothing would so astonish us as encountering a one-eyed man who assigned his half sight to his effort to achieve sexual purity, or a handless woman who confessed her mutilation to be self-inflicted in the pursuit of chastity.

It cannot properly be held that in what Jesus said (Matt. 5:27-30) we have a full treatment of this ageless problem. What he did say, however, is of great importance. Our primordial parents in Eden are thought by some (notably Augustine) to have been the cause of an identification of cohabitation and rebellion. The Manichees, to whose doctrines Augustine held in his pre-Christian days, said bluntly that sex is sin. Augustine the Christian said that the human generative process is evil; all men, therefore, have their natural origin because of a sinful act. Thus sin is by nature communicated from generation to generation. If we are confined to this understanding, there would seem to be valid ground for the criticism that Christian dogma has tended to make of sexual intercourse an inherently evil and ugly thing.

We will not argue with either Augustine or this criticism. Our concern is to point out that what Jesus knew to be in man seems to lie outside both the despair of Augustine and the ill temper of his critics. If our guidance is to come from the passage in Matthew, it is manifest that Jeus did not hold sex in scorn. Had he done so, would he not in dealing with adultery have suggested not the minor dismemberments of eye and hand but a radical glandular operation? Or since, as has been said, sexual intercourse is a matter between friends, would he not have been wise to make woman man's greatest enemy and vice versa? He had urged that making a friend was the best way of getting rid of an enemy. Why not say that in this case making an enemy was the best way of getting rid of a friend who was an accomplice in concupiscence?

No; lust is to adultery what anger is to murder. Each is the undirected release of a natural endowment which when disciplined is in the former the impulse to creativity and in the latter the impulse of power. Sex under control creates new individuals; anger under control creates a new society. Take either away or brand them both as inherently corrupt, and human life as we know it would end. Nothing would seem to be clearer than that Jesus believed man by lust could cast himself into hell, but that he thought man because of sex was doomed to hell is a complete misunderstanding of his recorded words.

In this connection the words of Jesus in Matt. 19:12 are instructive. The relation of marriage to chastity had been raised and puzzled his friends. Jesus himself seems to exhibit some indecision since the precept he cited was to be received by "only those to whom it is given." There follows the strange reference to male sterility. It is sometimes congenital, sometimes inflicted by others, and sometimes self-administered, "for the sake of the kingdom of heaven."

Of this third group of *castrati* we have no record. In the third century Origen in a mood of pious ecstasy mutilated himself. He soon regretted his rashness, and because of it unsympathetic churchmen forever denied him the honors of the church he served so conspicuously. What we are sure of is that whatever Jesus thought of sex, he did not assign to it the sordid role some of his followers gave it. His equivocal conclusion to the conversation referred to was: "He who is able to receive this, let him receive it."

This does not settle the problem; it merely sets down something about the nature of man as we deduce it from our Lord's teaching. Adultery in its generic meaning connotes the corruption of a pure substance by a base one. It is time that we restored to the Christian witness its essential faith that sex per se is as pure as love; and because it provides man's highest physical ecstasy, it also affords his most intimate sense of sharing the divine energies of creation.

5

What of taking oaths? Here the matter is simple. These were the oaths not hurled in anger to intimidate but offered in deference in order to convince. "Do not swear at all.... Let what you say be simply 'Yes' or 'No'; anything more than this comes from evil." (Matt. 5:34, 37.)

What sort of evil? Inner corruption? I think not. Rather it would appear to be the evil of diffidence or self-distrust. The swearing of oaths has a long and not always creditable history. It even seems that Jehovah was thought compelled to swear oaths to his unbelieving people, and the admonition of Jesus to abjure the practice was certainly ignored by Paul. Therefore the good and true have indulged the practice as well as the dishonest and cynical. A distinguished jurist recently said that it was a fairly accurate estimate that 75 per cent of oaths taken in court were assumed to be fraudulent.

What was the oath designed to do? To bring to the support of one's statement an authority thought to be more impressive than the statement itself or the speaker. The authority of the oath was not only powerful; it was even punitive in case the oath was dishonest. Thus the Siberian peasant swears on the head of a dead bear, meaning that if he is lying, he expects to be eaten by a living one.

Was not Jesus saying, in effect, that man has a capacity for speaking what he believes to be the truth that needs not to be buttressed by the corroboration of mythical witnesses? Neither heaven, nor the earth, nor Jerusalem, nor your head, Jesus said, should be necessary props for one's inner integrity. Say yes; say no, and let it go. After all, blind as we may be to truth and limited though our understanding must necessarily be, what is more impressive when we meet it than a self-confident yes or no in response to a question or as the credential of honesty? Oaths, said Santayana, are the fossils of piety.

There is nothing here that takes issue with the obvious fact of man's partial and partisan knowledge or his deliberate dishonesty. Or that would propose that all checks on statements made and those who make them be abandoned to a fatuous belief that all we hear is true and that all men are honest or all are liars. That is as silly as bringing in George, the beard of the prophet, or the great horned spoon to substantiate what we say.

No; Jesus, who knew what was in man, testified to that core of inner confidence that could stand alone and speak with its own voice. He did not guarantee accuracy; he recognized integrity. And we believe that he must have felt that if it was allowed to speak unaccompanied by the phony authority of others, it would grow in inner power and in outer acceptance. We think it is important that he said this. Do we not too easily forget that the authority he exhibited was always that of the clear yes or the simple no? "Anything more than this comes from evil." Perhaps it was the unadorned confidence of plain speech that identified his authority as different from that of the scribes.

CHAPTER VI

The Fulfillment of Prophecy

It is interesting to note that the section of the Sermon on the Mount which deals with the moral problems of killing, adultery, and honesty—and to that extent appears to parallel the Decalogue's proscriptions in these areas—is followed by our Lord's interest in three matters that lie outside the field of law. Giving alms, praying, and fasting are hardly amenable to legal control. They might be said to be *in* the social complex where law is necessary but not *of* it. Does this give us an intimation as to what Jesus meant by his assurance that he had no intention of abolishing the prophets?

We must not lose sight of our goal. Because Jesus knew what was in man, he directed to his hearers the sort of instruction that fitted their need and to which they could respond. Otherwise his teaching would have been capricious and his following erratic if not indeed fanatical. The common people heard him gladly not because he flattered them but because he understood them. It is out of what he said to them that we are able to deduce what he thought of them. Thus emerges what we not improperly call his doctrine of man.

Now law is predicated on the necessity for impartiality. Hard cases make bad laws, says the judge. Partisan laws make hard cases, says the juror. Hence we insist that ours is a government of laws, not of men. Since, however, society changes, laws are obsolescent. They must be amended, abolished, or rewritten. Generally what happens is that more laws are added to existing codes with the result that they explicitly or implicitly modify or nullify obsolete statutes.

Man's behavior among his fellows is determined less by laws, most of which he knows nothing about, than by inner compulsions. He may know as little about these as he knows of law, but he is likely to understand that what he does that gets him out of line is caused by an inner turbulence he has been unable to pacify. Thus when Jesus talked of murder in terms of anger and adultery in terms of lust and honesty in terms of a lack of self-confidence, his hearers must have known what he was talking about. Thus was the law fulfilled. There were, we may assume, many other laws fulfilled by understanding comments that were due to his knowledge of the human heart, comments as the last verse of the Fourth Gospel quaintly puts it which "were every one of them to be written, I suppose that the world itself could not contain the books that would be written."

1

The disciplines of the spirit cannot be caught within even the finest mesh of law. It is of these that the religious experience is fashioned. The argument as to whether a man can be good (law-abiding) without religion (ritual observance) is largely frivolous, but the question of the relation of inner control to external act is crucial. The role of the prophet was played on this larger stage; or perhaps it would be more precise to say that prophecy, as it was observed within the culture of the Jews, served this more crucial need.

The prophet, and there were false and true prophets, undertook to sensitize the hearts of people who were responsive to law by either a placid, bovine acceptance or an angry repudiation. The true prophet insisted that the heart was necessary to the hand, the spirit to the act; the false prophet said that grapes *did* grow on thorns, or that there was no necessary correlation between idea and action. What the true spokesman of the Lord was saying was that religion is necessary to morality, though by this he did not mean what is said by some of the stuffy arguments about it today. Rivers of oil and inundation by the blood of thousands of slain beasts were massively impressive but massively impotent in cleansing the heart of its uncharitable, unjust, and faithless attitudes. They were powerless to produce figs from thistles.

"The law and the prophets were until John; since then the good news of the kingdom of God is preached." (Luke 16:16.) We do not understand that with John the function of the prophet as suggested above was abandoned. Indeed, as Jesus was announcing the good news, he was fulfilling the prophets. What we encounter, therefore, in the passage (Matt. 6:1-18) that succeeds his fulfillment of the law is in effect a fulfillment of prophecy as it centers on three basic exercises of the inner religious spirit. We have little reason for thinking that these were the only matters that were important, but these three lie in areas that are familiar to all who wish not only to observe the letter of the law but to respond to the judge who holds court in camera in every heart.

These three, as they are dramatized in the simple experiences of almsgiving, praying, and fasting, are representative of three dynamic spiritual energies with which we are endowed: the impulses to self-giving, to self-replenishment, and to self-discipline. It can hardly be said that this is the totality of religious experience, but it comprises a great deal of it. And the prophetic urge to make formal, legal adherence to statute a matter of the outward expression of a native inner compulsion has had no fuller treatment than is found in the simple words of him who knew what was in man. It is beyond credulity to claim that he would have spoken of these three vital spiritual energies if he had not believed in them as representative of man's true nature.

2

Giving alms is one way of responding to an urgency with which, so far as we know, we are born. There is an explanation of this in purely naturalistic terms, and it comes out as a reflexive physical device for mantaining both the individual organism and the species. This explanation is altogether legitimate since it recognizes that something happens that looks like self-giving. What would be difficult to accept would be a refusal to admit any such impulse. The assimilative processes that nourish life are balanced by the donative processes that save life from surfeit or suffocation. Man lives to give and gives to live.

This is a favorite theme of poetry: the clouds *give* rain to the earth, the earth *gives* nutriment to the plant, the plant *gives* flowers to the gardener, and the corsage *gives* delight to the girl friend. For all it is poetic, it is not the less true. And when Jesus talked to his friends about "practicing your piety," he assumed that giving alms was something they all naturally wanted to do. He warned them, not against thinking that they had this impulse; he did not tell them to mistrust or repress it; he told them to protect it against blight.

How are we to understand this in terms other than those used by the naturalist? At once cognate words come to mind. That our language has been generous in the supply may mean that the expression of the self-giving impulse has been both universal and varied. To give alms is to pity, to feel compassion, to protect and defend, to sympathize, to be humane, merciful, to nurture, and to love. The list can be extended, but the point is clear: something within the human spirit tends to respond to people and situations that need human help.

This is so ordinary a circumstance as to excite far less notice than it deserves. It is when this self-giving impulse is deliberately repressed by one's self or some external factor that we sit up and take notice. The priest and Levite who averted their eyes from the bloody figure by the Jericho road are not excused as having no native sympathy for suffering. They

THE FULFILLMENT OF PROPHECY

actually were priests because they were dedicated to the offices of religion; therefore their aversion must have been, we may assume, due to preoccupation or worse. But whatever the cause, it is they, rather than the robbers, who are the villains of the story. Similarly it was Samaritan sympathy that identifies the hero, a compassion stronger than the superficialities of race and relgious prejudice. This was almsgiving—self-giving. It is the monopoly of none; it is the endowment of all. Why, therefore, we may ask, did Jesus include the merciful among the blessed? Because, we may reply, the impulse to give one's self voluntarily in response to demands that often are onerous and persistent *is* a blessing. Think for a minute what sort of life we would be doomed to suffer if compassion, mercy, sympathy, and their related moods were suddenly canceled. They are of such high potency in the mind of Jesus that he even admonished that they be used on one's enemies. It is likely that the first definition of God we ever heard was: God is love. To our more mature understanding this means God is self-giving; God gives alms.

But when we give alms, as Jesus puts it, we need to be careful. "Beware of practicing your piety before men." It is of itself interesting that he did not warn against transgressions of the *law* but did warn against *religious* malpractice. Clearly killing it so dramatic that it hardly needs to have a warning directed against it. But why warn against religious practices? Was it because religion has such low visibility and is so undramatic that it invites misuse, or, conversely, its correct practice demands a delicacy of sensitiveness that to the spiritually clumsy or obtuse is difficult? Observe, for example, in the *New York Times* of January 19, 1953, a dispatch from Washington appeared which said:

Carpenters raced against time in a remote corner of the National Guard Armory here today to complete an added starter to the procession of floats in Tuesday's Inaugural Parade. To the three men who conceived the idea it is known as "God's Float." They hope it will come to be known as such throughout the world. . . . Officials decided that this—the last float cenceived—should be first in the order of march. . . . In Gothic script on the sides and ends of the float will appear the legends, "Freedom of Worship" and "In God We Trust."

Beware!

Thus the self-giving impulse needs warning. So delicate a flower of the spirit can be dwarfed, mildewed, withered. Indeed, the margin between the impulse to *give* one's self and to *gratify* one's self is so razor-edged that—as Jesus put it —giving alms may be nothing more than getting the praise of men. Again it needs to be said that the desire for praise, insofar as it represents the wish to be accepted by one's fellows, is blameless; but by what subtle change it becomes a morbid craving for adulation, most of us know.

When it does, what happens? The normal and ingenuous impulse becomes a dishonest pose. The hyperbole of Jesus both amuses and admonishes. Picture a generous-hearted man with a trumpet lifted to his lips, his cheeks distended with the wind that was to herald a casual benefaction. The first blast turns his beneficence into buffoonery and fools no one except perhaps himself. He is a hypocrite and gets the hypocrite's reward. Unhappily, however, it is this masquerade that tends to sour the modest generosity that would conceal from one hand what the other is doing. God, we are assured, acknowledges *that* with soundless applause.

The point of all this is clear: the impulse to give one's self is innate and genuine; upon it rests the chance of mitigating much of life's wretchedness. It is not to be disdained as egotism or repressed as improvidence; it is a divine fragment in the human soul and must be protected against vulgarity and dishonest display.[1]

3

"When you pray": here we find ourselves confronting another impulse of the soul that cannot be caught within the plexus of code but against which we find Jesus uttering a word of caution. When giving is demanded by law, it is taxation; and few sound a trumpet before the collector of internal revenue when they pay. Giving can be demanded and remain an exercise of the soul only when the demand comes in the form of a human need that can be voluntarily met or refused. Similarly the law cannot require that we pray. It may compel a genuflection, but no threat can unlatch the door of the heart.

Now we have observed that almsgiving is one way by which the inherent impulse to give the self is manifest. It is native to the spirit; it is as universal as humanity. A naturalistic explanation takes nothing from its deep spiritual importance. As we study the experience of prayer, we encounter a similar circumstance. Just as one must by inner compulsion give of one's self, so one must because of a sense of inner depletion seek replenishment. If there were no self-giving, there would be no need for prayer.

This seems to limit the meanings we have allowed to attach themselves to the word. Unlike almsgiving prayer has no cognate except *petition* and its cognates—entreaty, supplication, begging. Praise, contemplation, adoration, worship, are all involved in our practice of prayer; but these are ac-

---

[1] Cf. Karl O. Kurth, *Documents of Humanity* (New York: Harper & Brothers, 1954). In the foreword Schweitzer says: "In my judgment this volume is one of the most significant to appear in modern times . . . a living testament of human kindness and compassion which some of the exiles (of German extraction) in their flight and anguish experienced when they encountered men and women of enemy nations."

cessory not essential to the idea. Prayer means asking for something.

Once again we see that this, like almsgiving, has a naturalistic explanation. Parallel to the giving need of the organism is the getting need. It must assimilate in order that it may give. If the balance between outgo and intake is not maintained, life is threatened. So also prayer: prayer is the replenishment of the self; it is to almsgiving what disgestion is to discharge, what anabolism is to catabolism.

This ought to be clear when we recall that in the Beatitudes we discover that it is the poor in spirit who are blessed; it is those who hunger and thirst after righteousness that are filled. Filled with what? With that, in a manner of speaking, which has been exhausted. We need not be puzzled by the suggestion that one may spend one's whole inventory of righteousness and discover a need for a refill. Jesus seems to have thought it possible; he may, indeed, have experienced it. And what, we may ask, is the essence of cynicism? The cynic is no fool; he is one who has run out of righteousness. Fill him up again, and he's a different man. This, to be sure, is the language of metaphor; but it is not for that reason obscure. Prayer is the process of spiritual replenishment; and the source of fullness is the Holy Spirit, promised to those who seek his infilling. But the impulse is our own; God, it would seem, does not go about with a gauge measuring the level of our spiritual supplies and bringing them up to capacity while we are away for the week end.

Furthermore prayer, like self-giving, suffers blight. The hypocrite against whose public praying Jesus warned is the same character who recently showed up with a trumpet and a handout. Then he wanted to be praised; now he simply wants to be seen. And seen he certainly is, but to what purpose? Does it replenish his soul? It will flatter his ego, but that's a different matter. No; it supplies him with nothing because, being a pretender, demanding replenishment is dissembling an emptiness he does not feel.

Prayer has another horrible example: the Gentile. Unlike the hypocrite, he is less concerned with being seen than heard. After all how can one know that another is praying simply by looking at him? But if he hears him, and hears his "much speaking," there is definitive proof of piety. And yet Jesus says "no" to the pretentious filibuster. Why? Obviously because the words fail to serve the purpose of the essential nature of prayer. "I thank thee that I am not like other men," prayed the Pharisee. Replenishment of the impoverished or hungry spirit is what prayer is; to say many words about that is literally a waste of breath. "Your Father knows what you need before you ask him." (Matt. 6:8.) He knows that the hungry soul must be fed. Few things would seem to be less necessary than a long speech by a beggar on the importance of an ample and balanced diet when he was so weak his hands could hardly lift up his suppliant bowl. It is clear that the visibility of the almsgiver and the filibuster of the prayermaker are alike irrelevant.

Of course the familiar metaphor of God in a secret room to which access is gained only by a door is in the same vein as the secret that the right hand keeps from the left. Jesus would have been quick to say to anyone who took him literally that God was as accessible outside as inside the room. After all it is impossible to keep anything concealed from the eye of God; what was therefore necessary was that other human eyes and ears should not corrupt the silent dialogue of replenishment. It is not to find God that we go inside and shut the door; it is to separate ourselves from eavesdroppers and gossips.

Blessed are the poor in spirit. All religions have an important place for prayer. Much that goes by the name is far from the experience of self-replenishment. Yet it is precisely because the soul's fatigue is so universal and so debilitating that the rituals of its restoration have become so elaborate. And, we might add, so futile. The fluttering prayer wheel and the fingered rosary and their countless variants all spring from the same central impulse in the soul. And because no man can live without giving the largesse of his compassion, and pity, and concern—as Wordsworth put it,

> such, perhaps,
> As have no slight or trivial influence
> On that best portion of a good man's life,
> His little, nameless, unremembered, acts
> Of kindness and of love—.[2]

so also men have devised ways for spiritual refreshment that have slight or trivial relation to religion. Are we not increasingly told that the exhaustion that these nerve-straining years have brought us is to be relieved best by barbiturates and alcohol? It is a long way from hunger and thirst for righteousness to the sleeping pill before bed; "thou at the end of a busy day enter the nearest cocktail lounge" may be the best some think they can do to mitigate tedium or weariness. But the need for relief is there in every soul. No self-giving without self-replenishment, but beware lest the impulses that activate both the gift and the prayer are corrupted by the delights of acclaim or the glances of the admiring. It is important that Jesus saw this in man. It is God's gift to him—never fully used, never wholly withdrawn.

The model prayer which follows needs little substantial comment here. It is enough to point out that its essence is petitional. This does not imply that it is selfish. On the contrary. It is the sort of prayer the depleted soul—the poor in spirit—might be expected to pray. One symptom of spiritual

[2] "Lines Composed a Few Miles Above Tintern Abbey."

fatigue is distrust. It is when we are tired that we tend to distrust our fellows; it is when our spirits are low that we doubt God and ourselves. Therefore the first petition asks that God's name be hallowed. Because something has happened not to God but to the empty heart. Also one needs to be reassured that God's purposes—his kingdom—will come. How quick we are to doubt this when our spiritual threshold is low. Because something has happened not to God's will and his kingdom but to us.

Another symptom of the spirit's exhaustion is anxiety. The spiritually robust is little disturbed about the morrow, but debilitation makes one anxious about all one's resources. Hence the prayer for bread. Not only does anxiety make its demands for bread; it is similarly concerned for moral strength that will enable one to stand up against temptation and the solicitations of evil. And nothing is more characteristic of low spirits than a sense of guilt. There is, of course, the danger that high spirits may deaden one's sense of moral failure; nevertheless the prayer for forgiveness issues from the heart that feels emptied of forgiveness. Properly enough our Lord comments that only as one forgives (self-giving) is one forgiven (God-replenished). It is the sick, the empty soul that tries to nourish itself on grudge, spite, hostility; it is the weary soul spent in forgiving others that may know the fullness of the forgiveness of God.

4

"And when you fast": this is the third religious exercise. It would seem to find its place in a logical sequence: first, the inner impulse to self-giving; second, the inner impulse to self-replenishment; and third, the impulse to bring these and all other native inner compulsions under self-discipline.

Here again we are struck by the fact that Jesus saw in man a capacity to discipline himself. This by no means indicates that success in self-control is guaranteed. The limits of the capacity for self-discipline are severely restricted. Jesus spoke with authority, and that is another way of saying he spoke under discipline; but he also said to Philip, "The words that I say to you I do not speak on my own authority; but the Father who dwells in me does his works" (John 14:10). This divine supplement is available to all who lack the full capacity of self-control; but that it is to be had only by those who seek it—and seeking it is an act of self-discipline—is in itself witness to this component of soul without which personal religion would be impossible. To say that I am the captain of my soul should properly mean that I am a commissioned officer. It does not say that I shall be able by myself to pilot my craft through all the buffetings of tide and tempest, but it should mean that I shall not abandon my ship no matter how long the passage or how savage the sea.

The act of self-discipline which our Lord uses to illustrate the point is fasting. This did not mean a low-calorie diet at the demand of one's vanity or one's doctor. It is something almost universally practiced by religious individuals excepting perhaps by pious Christians and comes from the idea that somehow the flesh is mischievous in its effects on the soul. Much evidence supports this: the saint is ascetic, the sinner a glutton; what Milton called "carnal mirth" was the opposite of the rapture of the contemplative. The notion that the measure of one's Godliness is in direct ratio to the measure of one's girth is pretty generally accepted though, it must be conceded, it does not conspicuously affect our behavior. On the contrary we have a real fondness for the Friar of Orders Gray in the old English ballad who said:

> Myself, by denial, I mortify
> With a dainty bit of a warden pie;

and,

> After supper, of heaven I dream,
> But that is fat pullet and clouted cream.

But fasting, as much as anything else, is a symbol of self-discipline, for the essence of discipline is denial. Once more we turn back to the Beatitude offered the meek. Blessed are the disciplined, as the word was interpreted there. It is easy to see its opposite in other terms: Unfortunate are the self-indulgent, for instead of inheriting the earth, they lose all they have. This impulse of self-discipline, like the other two impulses that have been discussed, has an explanation in naturalistic terms. Discipline—or denial—is imposed on all organisms by the exigent pressures of environment; the growth of the inclination and the capacity of the human individual to discipline himself is the process of physical and psychological maturation. It is the child who cries for the extra dessert; it is the mother who denies herself in order that her infant may eat. No discipline, no growth; no self-discipline, no spiritual adulthood.

Thus the self-disciplining impulse is native to the soul, but it needs to be protected. As fasting was used to induce a state of mind hospitable to spiritual influences, Jesus seems to have approved it. Somehow we do not find him fasting, though the rigors of his self-discipline must have been apparent to all who knew him. And once again it is the hypocrite who mocks the intention of self-denial. We first heard him blowing a trumpet; then we saw him bowed in devotion at a street intersection; now he appears looking dismal and disfigured, and his "fasting may be seen by men." Men *do* see him; and he has his reward and, we hope, presently goes home to eat a hearty meal.

Disguise your fasting, says Jesus; keep your hair tidy and your face clean. This is not to deceive the passer-by, to strike a pose that is dishonest. It is rather to correct the idea that self-discipline is unnatural, that it must be advertised by a disheveled head and a dirty face and by its very disorderliness misrepresent itself. Insofar as fasting was intended to reflect the denial or discipline of self as devotion to God, it should be made, said Jesus, as natural as true devotion, which is relaxed, decorous, and cosmetic. God will not miss it; and you, to say the least, will be more presentable in public.

We may feel, as many clearly do, that self-discipline is no fun. This is why Jesus' use of fasting as its religious symbol is so apt. Since it is often irksome, we easily deceive ourselves by ingenious subterfuge; blessed are those who hunger and thirst so we will achieve blessedness by making ourselves wretched. The surfeited go to sleep saying their prayers, so we will do without our supper and dream of a heaven of clouted cream. Because the truly disciplined person is most truly mature, most of us must see ourselves as adolescent, that stage in our psychological growth that is perhaps the most tumultuous since it provides the transition between the discipline of others and the acceptance of self-discipline. This is easy for neither party; parents are often as resentful at the assertion of independence as the child is afraid of it. The transfer, however, must be made. It must not be concealed by hypocrisy or delayed by fear. It is man's gift; he is not foredoomed to tyranny of any sort—inner or outer. He must fast; he must deny himself; he must set rules and observe them. These are truly divine prerogatives; little wonder that we find it easier to remain dependent or to regress to the simplicities of childhood.

"Do not look dismal, like the hypocrites, for they disfigure their faces that their fasting may be seen by men." But in positive form the admonition might read: Discipline yourself, for to do this has been given you in a divine endowment, but be careful of your inclination to display how disciplined you are. God needs it not, and it is the business of nobody else. And he who makes a display of his self-discipline is more likely than not covering up a deep sense of forced dependence on others that is hateful to him. How profoundly Jesus knew what was in man!

CHAPTER VII

The Proverbs of Jesus

We have been concerned with the ways in which Jesus fulfilled prophecy. He brought to bear on three basic spiritual impulses clear warnings as to how they could be corrupted by insincerity. The giving of self, the quest for replenishment of the soul, the exercise of self-discipline, were all indispensable to the vital spirit; none of them could be demanded or regulated by law. It was the chief concern of the prophet to sharpen the spiritual sensitiveness of those who held these endowments lightly or in disdain.

1

We think it significant that the breath from the mountain eddied about some other aspects of human experience that are not amenable to law and, if they are a concern of prophecy, would seem to have been caught in too fine a mesh. In a manner of speaking they appear to be more peripheral than central; and yet they have become more familiar, if anything, than some of the matters that have engaged us. Why is this? They do not carry with them inherent moral compulsions or correlative penalties; they are advisory rather than mandatory; they are the sententious wisdom generally called "proverbs." Proverbs are epigrammatic observations on life; they are not rules or rubrics. They state a proposition and indicate what happens when it is accepted or ignored. To differentiate them from legal or prophetic writings, they are called in the Bible wisdom literature. More simply they might be called common sense. "The eye is the lamp of the body. So, if your eye is sound, your whole body will be full of light." (Matt. 6:22.) "The spirit of man is the lamp of the Lord, searching all his innermost parts." (Prov.

20:27.) The similarity of form and intention in these Old and New Testament sayings is manifest.

What is important for this study, however, is that these proverb-admonitions tell us a great deal about what Jesus saw in man. Proverb making is an old art, and good proverbs are important literary vehicles. For this reason we have all sorts. The cynical realism of Zarathustra reflects the view of Neitzsche on life; the *Analects* of the urbane sage of Chou tells us what Confucius saw as he surveyed the human scene. Benjamin Franklin, sagacious and whimsical; *Mein Kampf* peppered with Hitler's sardonic and savage judgments. What we discover is not so much that proverbs are true or false as that they are reflections of one individual's views of man and society. Proverbs neither present nor ask for proof; they neither argue nor threaten. For this reason very often they reveal as much about the author as about the idea he has compressed into aphorism.

To say this in no way reduces their value. Their invasion of colloquial speech is proof enough of their worth and their common sense. How aptly they illumine human frailty and foolishness; how gaily they report our wisdom and our nobility! Jesus looked at life, we have every reason for believing, with singular steadiness and penetration; and when he spoke of it, his words floated on a deep tide of understanding of man, man the image of God, man in fellowship with all the sons of men.

2

"Where your treasure is, there will your heart be also." (Matt. 6:21.) This is the proverb that closes the short homily on the danger of acquisitiveness. It is characteristic of Jesus' aphorisms that they are embedded in a simple homily about a common experience. And it is interesting to note that it is the proverb we remember and repeat with approval, while at the same time—if we take the trouble to think about it—we repudiate the homily which it summarizes. His comment about avarice or, to put it more ingratiatingly, about saving we totally ignore. Who of us in the practice of Christian virtue is careful to keep the larder, the closet, and the purse empty? We do not regard Jesus' admonition as a command, though we acknowledge the risks that plague the hoarder and the hoard. Perhaps we think we have blunted his suggestion by inventing thief-proof vaults (and insurance against theft), insecticides, and stainless steel. Heaven, we agree, should be proof against light fingers, Lepidoptera, and ferric oxide; so since we have developed pretty good protection on earth, we will go ahead and lay up near at hand treasures for ourselves. Beyond this, indeed, we come a great deal closer to thinking that improvidence instead of thrift is sinful. Nevertheless who will deny that where our treasure is, there will our heart be also?

This is a spiritual fact that cannot be changed by external factors, for it is a response that is made to man's capacity to assess and pursue values. The object of one's desire is neither constant nor consistent, and the treasure we seek is as varied as our hearts. And yet psychologically we have no way of denying the heart the satisfaction it feels in holding close what it possesses. Moral considerations do not alter the fact: a man's heart is as much in ill-gotten gain as it is in his legitimate rewards. What he treasures may even be as worthless as dust; but if you want to find his heart, look for his treasure.

Since it is obvious that this sort of thing lies outside the effective direction of law, we wonder why Jesus spoke of it. Our efforts to perfect protective devices for the things that are valuable to us are not wholly wasted nor are they wicked. Indeed, they represent in some areas human wisdom and ingenuity of the highest quality. The quick answer is that he saw hearts attached to values that were easily lost. When one loses what one loves, one literally loses heart. If men could see and seek what values are durable beyond any possible damage, they would be spared the anguish of loss. This is simple common sense. But deeper than this is the realization that man is a value-seeker; he sees alternatives and makes choices, he builds for himself scales of value, and thus is able to put together the things that we call in the aggregate culture. He is not, in other words, destined to accept in the realm of values any one choice. This is one aspect of the awesome fact of human freedom; and whether he be sage or fool, he will deposit in his heart treasury the things he thinks are worthful and defend them with his life. We may argue —if we think there is value in it—whether a materialistic or a spiritual wealth index is better; but there is no argument as to where the heart of the materialist and his enigmatical opposite is to be found. Munificence and miserliness alike reflect what a man has in his heart.

3

"If then the light in you is darkness, how great is the darkness." (Matt. 6:23.) This proverb is less familiar perhaps than the one about treasure, but it is one of the most discerning of our Lord's comments about the human spirit. There is no assurance that we are born with sound eyes; if we were, we might be confident about our total illumination. "*If*," he says: "if your eye is sound"—the element of contingency is important, for it is set over against any possible interpretation of life in terms of fate.

More important, I think, is the observation he is making about one of the subtlest of human failures. He is a rare person—if indeed he exists at all—who honestly believes that his "body" is "full of darkness." Contrition, the sense of guilt and of failure, is a dark experience to which the illumined spirit will confess; but he confesses it because he thinks he is full of the light that casts its dark shadow. But the most troublesome sort of person is he who, self-deceived about the deep-lying motives of his soul, prates noisily about light which in reality is darkness.

Thus the man who struggles with a hidden sense of inferiority boasts about his complete adequacy. The light he casts is, in the vivid metaphor of Jesus, darkness. Or the mother who, resisting the oppressive sense of rejection by her growing children, beams with oversolicitude. Or the preacher who, to disguise a gnawing avarice that he dares not confess, rails righteously at the injustices of the economic order and its grasping protectors. In effect we have here from the lips of him who knew what was in man a warning that all of us need and that too few of us heed. The mind, which is the symbol of the light that is in us, is preternaturally clever in concealing from us the things within us that we cannot face up to. This gives us false security, saves us from self-rebuke, creates an image of the self that pleases, gives us a status with ourselves that we do not have, or deserve, with others. What this sort of mischief does for us is spelled out by those who have to deal with sick minds. And yet all that they can say to us has its summary in the description Jesus gives of such individuals. The light in them is darkness. How great it is! he exclaims. So great indeed that it convinces the shadowed soul that it is suffused with radiance.

Once more we are reminded that this is something not amenable to law or code. To exhort against it is futile, for the mind will put up its resistance. "We must distrust," said Daniel Webster in rebuking one of these dark-light individuals. "We must distrust our instinct for intervention, for the wish to have one's own will prevail often disguises itself under a mask of solicitude." Eloquently put but no more pointedly than the more familiar words of a more famous person.

4

"You cannot serve God and mammon." (Matt. 6:24.) Everybody knows this, but few of us believe it. It sounds dogmatic, arbitrary; but since we think that Jesus had a right to his opinion, we agree to let him say it so long as he does not try to compel our acceptance or practice of the idea.

Well, obviously he was not laying down a law; he was passing judgment on man's futile effort to divide himself between two competing loyalties. Having seen it tried, he judged that it was impossible. "No one can"; "you cannot"; that is final. There is no hint of censoriousness or threat here, no mawkish disappointment in human failure. The proverb needs no tub-thumping emphasis, for it is as simple as this: one plus one equals one; one plus two equals nothing —the arithmetic of loyalty. You and God; you and mammon; but not you and God and mammon.

These odd equations rest on two basic facts; the human individual has a right to choose his own loyalties. Just as his heart is where his treasure is, his happiness—and to a degree his security—is where his loyalty is. The second fact is that the soul has not resource enough to offer its dominant loyalty to more than one. It is clear from the context of this proverb that the masters referred to are opposites, as opposite as God and mammon. *Mammona* in general meant wealth and was personified as the Roman deity Pluto to represent something more dramatic than accumulated gold. Mammon was a god as Pluto was a god. It is instructive to learn that in both Greek and Roman mythology Pluto was the god of the lower world and that plutocracy, from *ploutos,* means the rule of the rich. We may make our own inferences.

There is no necessity for implying that Jesus was using

mammon in its mythological context, though there is no assurance that he was not. But it is certain that he was thinking of God and mammon, the "two masters" he referred to, as exclusive opposites. No problem arises if we have two masters—or half a dozen indeed—who are all the same kidney. Thus one may be loyal to one's parents and one's wife and children without falling into the alternate moods of love and hate, devotion and scorn. Similarly one can serve his community and his church and his school and his business without necessarily becoming involved in conflict.

But that is not where our difficulty lies. The ambivalence of love and hate that we feel for those we are closest to is, if properly understood, a wholesome tension. Our troubles begin when we try to draw into the circle of our devotion focuses of loyalty that are essentially uncongenial or divisive. This, says Jesus, cannot be done, for loyalty to one becomes disloyalty to another, and that sort of ambivalence creates more than tension; it ignites explosion.

We may assume that this common-sense judgment of Jesus was reached by observing the behavior of those about him. We may even assume, indeed, that it grew out of his own experience, for the third temptation was clearly an effort of the evil one to divide Jesus' loyalty between the Father and him. Nowadays we call this singleness of devotion "integration" and assign to it almost all our conspicuous successes. Jesus, who always did the things that were pleasing to the Father, knew the rewards of constant and undivided love. But it was a loyalty that he chose for himself; and as he looked at his human brethren, he saw the same rewards and penalties waiting their choice that attended his own.

5

"Sufficient unto the day is the evil thereof." (Matt. 6:34 K.J.V.) This is the familiar summary of the famous homily on anxiety. First off it may seem a gloomy comment or an empty platitude. Everyone knows there's enough evil—whether it be bad luck or stupidity or clumsiness or malice—allocated "unto the day." Furthermore there is no satisfaction in the fact. On the contrary we feel that there is much too much, and it is *that* that needs emphasis in our bedeviled world. We want the amount diminished, not accepted.

Why then did he not exhibit a more cheerful mood and have something to say about the good? Because to say "sufficient unto the day is the good thereof" isn't true. There is a point at which evil becomes intolerable; there is too much of it. But is there a point at which good piles up a surplus and becomes a burden? No; for the moment good becomes intolerable as surfeit or surplus, it ceases to be good and becomes a part of the "evil thereof."

Consequently this proverb is no reflection of a dour spirit; it is good common sense and will, we may assume, be accepted as such by both the anxious and the relaxed. The anxious will say that enough evil is enough; the contented will say that enough is not too much.

It is therefore not with the proverb that we have trouble; it is with the homily that it summarizes. To a casual reading we seem to be told that we must be unconcerned with food, drink, and clothing because the birds and the lilies get along without worrying. To which the impatient rejoinder is that since we are not of the flowering and feathering species, we cannot expect to enjoy their immunities. Thus the words of Jesus about anxiety would tend, if we acted like birds and lilies, to exaggerate the day's evil rather than abate it. Imagine after a pious resolution to make no preparation for breakfast fluttering to a neighbor's door and explaining, birdlike, that we expected to be fed at his table.

No; Jesus was indulging no such fantasy. He was, on the

contrary, adding the problem of anxiety to the problem of divided loyalty just discussed. Is it not the necessity we feel for distributing our concerns in such a way as will cover all our needs—or our loyalties to our health and security—that is the cause of much of our anxiety? One would not need to worry if there were not so many responsibilities involved in getting through the day. Because we cannot respond to the demands of all our little gods and the little mammons, we become anxious. The Greek word for "anxious" (*merimnao*) means literally "dividing the mind."

Now anxious people are, as Jesus put it, "men of little faith" (Matt. 6:30). Or to put it otherwise, the more faith we have, the less anxious we will be. This is true, we think, even though the extent of anxiety is greater in our times and the understanding of the deep causes of anxiety are more exact than in his day. For reasons he did not specify he seemed to think that the Gentiles were great worriers. Thus they were tireless in their pursuit of food, drink, and clothing. Today economists tell us that food and fibers are the basic concern of economic life. If our faith is in them, we shall be anxious or not in terms of our possession of them. And what if we are worried? It is not too great a strain on language to say that worry is the primary cause of war, inside and out.

He did not leave the matter thus; he provided an object of faith and quest. It was the same one specified in his aphorism about God and mammon. "Seek first his kingdom and his righteousness," for clearly loyalty to God is loyalty to his kingdom as anxiety for things is the result of loyalty to mammon. To some this may make life look too easy: just be good and hold out your hand. So it is realistically said that while we may think the kingdom is a grand idea, we had better make our regular trips to the supermarket just the same. We console ourselves that this is a harmless sort of faithlessness; at least we are hardly impressed that it constitutes disobedience to a divine command.

As indeed it does not. Jesus was talking not law and prophecy but common sense. We can be anxious if we want to and perhaps will be whether we want to or not, and our agitation may be seen in nothing more than biting our fingernails or in something as disturbing as the quick recoil of fear. And our psychiatrist will tell us the trouble started when we were tiny and felt rejected by our harassed father, who was too anxious about the mortgage to take time out for a romp with the kids. So it goes. And yet there is common sense here if we look closely enough at it. What is basic to the kingdom of God and his righteousness? Is it not a quality of spirit in all those who seek it—and by seeking find it—that is more concerned about the well-being of others than one's own? And is not the righteousness of God the righteousness of mutuality, compassion, concern, or—in the best of all possible words—love? And is it not true that love begets love, that the concern of one excites reciprocal concern in another, and that if I am "anxious" for the rewards of the kingdom for you, you will be anxious that all these things shall be mine as well? That is as much warranty as we need.

This is not double talk; if it sounds like it, it may be because we live in a society that is geared to a very different kind of seeking. We seem to be trying to fill an emotional vacuum, to reimburse ourselves for a loss or a lack of inner resource. Disappointment, frustration, and anxiety inevitably result because, ironically, there are literally not enough of the rewards of the gentile quest to provide us with a sense of security. We are, in a word, "Gentiles," endlessly seeking things and promising ourselves that when we have enough good for the day, the evil will vanish. This throws the idea of Jesus into reverse and points out exactly why ours is the most anxiety-ridden of all the ages of recorded time. Jesus knew what was in man, how anxious he is and why. Man is not fated to it; there have been many spirits whose contentment was incandescent; and if the light that is in us is not darkness, we too can glow. We have no record of Jesus in an anxious frame of mind, an anxiety, that is, that concerned his personal fortunes. It is not sentimentality to say he had a birdlike freedom, a flowerlike tranquillity; it is solid fact to say that he sought first the Father's kingdom and his righteousness. Is not the former the result of the latter? And he said it could similarly be true of us. "Let the day's own trouble be sufficient for the day." (Matt. 6:34.)

6

"Judge not, that you be not judged." (Matt. 7:1.) Here is familiarity again. To be faithful to the epigram's intention, we should add the reason for the withheld judgment: "for with the judgment you pronounce you will be judged."

There are several things to be said here. First, to take this literally is quite impossible. It is hardly possible not to judge others. The Greek work is *krino,* which gives us a rich variety of meanings and kin words that run all the way from the simple matter of dis*crim*ination to in*crim*ination, from crisis to criticism (meaning censoriousness). But if by a mighty heave at our bootstraps we could lift ourselves to a level of complete indifference or relaxed tolerance, we should not escape the judgment of others thereby. Their discernment will judge the quality of our restraint, if they call it that; or will impugn our equivocation, if they call it that. But there is, nevertheless, a shrewd judgment in this admonition, namely, that if you attend strictly to your own business, you are less likely to invite the imputations of others. Beyond that it is hardly possible to go. Jesus was pointing out that action on this level is reciprocal: "the measure you give will be the measure you get." Give none, get none.

The second thing is that in the business of judging others hypocrisy has a field day. Jesus warned against this bad actor in other connections, but in the area of passing judgment his opportunity for histrionics was boundless. It is almost impossible not to strike a pose when giving out with an opinion. We like to appear pained, disappointed, shocked, condescending, or indignant. This is because posture is important to pronouncement. Even the austerity of the judge *looks* like an affectation. Because judges are supposed to be sober, they must act solemnly even though they are inwardly agitated by amusement or outrage.

The third comment is that there is canny shrewdness in the observation that most of our effort at judging others is frustrated because of something that distorts or blinds our vision. It is a log in the eye. This gay exaggeration is part of the mood of the proverb maker, and we may imagine that our Lord indulged the extravagance with a smile. But how true it is that we only see part of what we look at.

Once again we have here a simple statement of a truism of modern psychology. What is more characteristic of censoriousness than that one finds distasteful in others what one will not admit is characteristic in one's self? The man who criticizes the puffy ostentation of another puffs as he protests, and the niggard is always quick to whine about the miserliness of another. This is what Jesus meant by being judged by the judgment we pronounce. He could have made it even more pointed by saying that in the very act of judging another one judges one's self. Judgment is not only reciprocal; it is reflexive.

The mote and beam dialectic is, I think, obvious humor, for we have here no mandate, no law; we have whimsical common sense. Just as we can be anxious if we wish and pay the consequences, so also we can judge and be judged. Judgment understood as the exercise of one's powers of discernment and choice is, however, a very important matter. "Do not judge by appearances, but judge with right judgment." (John 7:24.) There is no contradiction here—rather a recognition of an important human prerogative that must be protected carefully against misuse. It is far from the idea that man cannot make choices or that if he makes them, they cannot alter a situation immutably fixed against human influences. So we find it is possible to see clearly and judge rightly after the log is taken out of one's own squinting eye. The speck in the other's eye is thereupon judged for what it is; and if in one's judgment it should be removed, the situation may be helped all along the line.

7

"Do not give dogs what is holy; and do not throw your pearls before swine, lest they trample them underfoot and turn to attack you." This unabridged statement of the more familiar "neither cast ye your pearls before swine" (K.J.V.) is not too long to be rated as a proverb. As in the others we have studied, we see a shrewd observation on life—a human foible pointed out and its consequences predicted.

We do well to be careful that we do not make these bright apothegms appear too pat either in their content or in their sequence. But it is at least interesting to note that there is a normal order in the two comments about judgment and pearls. The man who has no discernment of values is the man who throws pearls before swine. No other reasonable explanation can be offered for such erratic behavior. Nor does he have a very safe understanding of the state of mind of pigs when they discover what has been tossed to them is as inedible as it is invaluable. We are not sure that the porcine response to deception is always as vindictive as it seems here. But, then, this is an observation about people and pearls as well as about pigs, and we do know something about them.

We have for the most part forgotten the place of the dogs in this proverb. This may be because of our fondness for our canine companions; and while we treat them well, we do not give them what is holy, whatever that means. How dogs respond to such well-intentioned but foolish piety, we are not told. Perhaps they accept the holy thing with a soulful but puzzled look. They seem not disposed to resent it. But we dislike pigs as much as we love dogs, and this is what compounds the folly of throwing pearls before them.

This is, of course, metaphor; we may be properly skeptical that anyone in his right mind has ever done this sort of thing. Nevertheless the metaphor sharpens the fact of human folly and irresponsibility and warns us that the careless use or the callous misuse of the values that are ours results not only in their loss but in our destruction. The man who casts pearls before swine does not disappoint the pigs; he decrees his own death. We must not be too urgent in pressing the intimations of this proverb, but it is significant that in the matter of man's use of values Jesus makes room for what we call both the values of the spirit and the values of the thing. Presumably "what is holy" represents spiritual values as "pearls" are symbolic of material values.

These proverbs of Jesus are being used to gain some insight into what he saw in man, and I am inclined to leave this one with the final observation that it showed what man will sometimes do with the wealth he has and will do it willingly to his own hurt. Man is not stupid; he knows a pearl from a peck of corn; and if he tosses it into the pigsty, he is less foolish than mad. It is this fact, as one surveys the history of culture as Toynbee has, that makes one wonder about the future of our own. Other cultures have died partly because they wasted their wealth, not only of things but of the resources of the spirit. What is to be the result of our prodigal natural waste? What—and this is more searching—is to happen to us if we toss the spiritual riches of truth, and love, and freedom, and laughter, which are our inheritance, into the pigpen of war, and greed, and pride? Will they not turn again and rend us? This is not a pretty sight, but it is what should be called up every time we quote this familiar proverb. There was no whimsy in the picture of these pigs as there was in the brethren with the afflicted eyes. Nor are we allowed an option in the former case: of course we can judge if we wish and risk the reciprocal judgment, but here the hazard is too great. To be attacked by pigs is not only ignominious; it is fatal.

8

By far the most familiar of Jesus' proverbs is the Golden Rule. We have been often told that it is found in the lore of many religions. Some have gone so far as to say that it is in the area of ethical conduct all we know and all we need to know. Indeed, when Jesus added his commentary, his observation was that in this rudiment of wisdom all of the law and the prophets is summarized (Matt. 7:12). It takes very little imagination to see what would happen in the world if this rule were really *the* rule of conduct.

The brief homily that precedes the adage is similarly familiar. It would seem to be purposely cast in the mode of simple encouragement to the dispirited. So much of man's asking, seeking, and knocking appears to be met with the wrong answers, the wrong discoveries, and the wrong doors that it is easy to despair of getting the right ones. But the failure of quest and question is not to be taken as meaning that all ears are sealed against us, all roads are barred, all doors are bolted. The credential for our asking and knocking is that a man will not knowingly give a stone to one who asks for a loaf or a serpent to one who asks for a fish. This is true even of us "who are evil." [1] It would therefore appear that we are to assume that man's indigenous generosity, however enfeebled or denied, is to be made the a priori assumption on which we are to exercise our impulse to ask, seek, and knock.

Without this basic confidence the Golden Rule would be unsupportable, for it rests on the idea that people will respond to our generosity to them and try at least to reciprocate. The cynic who advises, Do to others what you think they will do to you but do it first, has too much in experience to support his grim counsel; but if it were the established rule of life, unimaginable desolation would long ago have overwhelmed human affairs. Though it takes a confidence more rocklike than simple optimism to act as Jesus suggests, this confidence is justified, I think, for four reasons.

First, this is calculated behavior; or if we like it better, we can call it calculated risk. There is nothing haphazard or capricious in behavior that rests on the choice of *what we want* before we act toward another—"*whatsoever* ye would." Second, this is in terms of what *we* want, not some imposed or compelled ideal or standard—"whatsoever *ye* would." Think what this means as it affects the relation between free choice and action. Third, it is in terms of what we *want*, not what we think is acceptable in terms of authority or amenity—"whatsoever ye *would*." Here is neither the sycophant's smile, the conformist's smirk, nor the weakling's

---

[1] It should hardly be necessary to say that this is not a summary judgment on human nature as it has sometimes been regarded. Translators, seeking to correct this misunderstanding, have rendered it: "You then, imperfect as you are" (Weymouth); "for all your evil" (Moffatt); "you, bad as you are," and so on. Even such aid as translators can give is hardly necessary in the light of the fact that the evil specified is disqualified as summary judgment because the evil person referred to knows "how to give good gifts." This means he is not wholly evil. Far from it!

whine; it is the response of a calculating and responsible mind to a human situation. Last, it is an attitude that rests only in action—"whatsoever ye would that men should do to you, *do*. . . ." "Do" is the power word in the rule.

Can it be said that it is these vital factors—calculation, personal desire, and action—that give the Golden Rule its universality? We have been told ever since men began behaving that what they wanted was to express themselves genuinely in their responses to one another, and that what they most resented was the imposition of authority or the inertia of inaction. Here, as though it were a direct answer to what we are now told is the demand of the modern generation, we have reciprocal behavior based on man's inner desires plus the demands of his sense of freedom and his necessity for personally directed action. Little wonder that this profound distillation of universal wisdom—the law and the prophets, as Jesus put it—is found in the ethical structure of all cultures. What does that seem to say about man? If this is true, by all means let us ask, seek, and knock.

9

"Wide is the gate, and broad is the way, that leadeth to destruction." (Matt. 7:13 K.J.V.) This is the form in which the adage is most familiar. We do not quote it much; it has the nagging clamor of a bell buoy, ceaselessly warning us against drifting out of the safe channel; it is the impertinence of traffic signs. Those who use it can make themselves unwelcome in gay company. It sounds almost like ranting, and we much prefer the more spacious words about abundant life as if that meant a capacious gate and a commodious highway.

Nevertheless there is common sense here as a full quotation

of the R.S.V. rendering will show.[2] This is not a philosophy of life; it is no distillation of all the factors of experience that go to make up the way, as life is called. We must not make the mistake of thinking that common sense is impertinent or gay or somber; its quality is that it is common, common to all experience. Underneath these simple words, then, we may expect to find some things that are alien to none of us.

The first thing is that the choices we make are our own; they are not the malign or beneficent compulsions of force or fate that not only send us where they will but contrive to deceive us into thinking that we are determining our own directions. Here is an area where argument has flashed and sputtered during all the long time of man's thinking. It is not yet foreclosed, nor is its termination likely. But we know which side Jesus took.

The second thing is that destruction is the terminus of the wide, easy way and that life is the end of the narrow, hard way. If the words "destruction" and "life" are not used to indicate postmundane finalities—for which in this context there is little warrant—they deal with circumstances with which we are all familiar. It *is* easier to drift than to direct ourselves; there *is* a sense of congenial roominess in the wide dimensions of irresponsibility, and there *are* many who "enter thereby." Indeed, there are times in the lives of us all when we slip the tether of restraint to breathe the roving air. Can it not be said of the "many," which includes us, that they spend most of their lives moving from one road to the other —turning from the broad one when destruction threatens and shifting back to it when the narrow one slows up traffic?

[2] "Enter by the narrow gate; for the gate is wide and the way is easy, that leads to destruction, and those who enter by it are many. For the gate is narrow and the way is hard, that leads to life, and those who find it are few." (Matt. 7:13-14.)

The third thing is that the narrow road that leads to life is not always easy to find, and therefore those who travel it are few. One reason it is narrow may be that it has to accommodate only a trickle of travelers.

Now it has been said that this is regarded by the big-gate and broad-road wayfarers as a gloomy comment on life, yet it is only another way of saying that self-discipline is onerous and most of us do our uttermost to avoid it. The consequences of this, however, cannot be evaded by those of us who try to shirk it: the refusal to discipline ourselves results in destruction either by no discipline at all which is destruction by diffusion, indecision, vacillation, temporizing, improvization, incoherence, and other such like destroyers; or by the compulsions of another which in essence is a denial of one's indefeasible right to do as he pleases. This is a shattering and immediate destruction; one might call it the negation of individuality. On the other hand, the narrow way means that the narrow mind or the isolated and obsessive interest leads to the opposite of destruction—called life. Some call it integration or integrity. Only as there is brought to life singleness of direction and assiduous cultivation of those things that advance the conscious intent, shall the vitality of the spirit or the integrity of individuality be protested.

To test the wisdom of this proverb, then, we need only look about us. It will not be difficult to find the traveler on the narrow way. There is nothing unsteady in his gait; there is no indecision in his eyes; there is no spurious joy in his heart. Call him a saint, a genius, a success, or whatever, he is easily identified. Or better than looking about us at others, we can look at ourselves, for it is at us that this proverb points. It is personal choice that we are exercising here, not a pressure to which we are yielding. That this is not a mandate is manifest, for the reason that self-discipline cannot be imposed. The moment external compulsion lays even a finger on self-discipline, it ceases to be self-discipline and becomes coercion, be it ever so gentle. So we have often chosen and will choose again the gate we want to enter and the road we want to travel, but we shall not deceive ourselves as to the destination we are headed for or the measure of true satisfaction our journeyings will bring us.

10

In "you will know them by their fruits" (Matt. 7:20) "them" means us, and there is no sentiment that evokes more general agreement than this. It is clear from the context within which this proverb is found that there were those who said that the relation between profession and action was *not* definitive. They were called false prophets, men, we assume, who were a degree worse than the hypocrites, for they were liars. The description Jesus gives is one of the most dramatic of all his characterizations of men. They "come to you in sheep's clothing"; their air of innocence and harmlessness disarms you. But when you put out your hand to caress the woolly head, there is the sudden flattening of the ears, the retracted lips, and the snap of sharp teeth; and your hand is snatched back lacerated and bloody. It must have been a deep sense of outrage that caused Jesus to depict these deceivers in such bitter simile. Was it merely his own hurt; had his hand been bitten by a masquerading wolf? Or was his concern a wider one?

Don't be too fastidious, these false prophets said. How can you be sure that grapes cannot be found on thornbushes or figs on thistleweed? At least the possibility is worth a chance. Good *may* come of evil; certainly it is clear even to the blind that evil sometimes comes from good. The correlations between right and wrong are not fixed; they are fluid. Nothing is more confusing than the effort to assign causes for effects in the area of conduct. Out of palpable evil some good has come; out of determined good—well, all men's motives are ambiguous, and the results of action are contingent, and the nature of man's devotion is ambivalent, and his emotions are unstable, not to say capricious. Thus spoke the wolf in sheep's clothing.

This is not unfamiliar; in confused times like our own it is given plausibility by much of the spectacle humanity is making of itself. And the result of it is a tendency to relax such rigidities as have hitherto controlled our behavior. Nevertheless one of the pillars on which our ethical structure rests is the principle that ends and means must be of the same moral mixture and that the moment that foundation crumbles our most secure support is gone.

The place to argue this point is not here. If we have come to the time when we think hate will sprout love in its thorny branches and from the brambles of war peace will bloom, we have already succumbed to the false prophet. Perhaps we actually think he is a sheep; worse, we may have greater fondness for him now that we know him as a wolf. In either case we are in for trouble: to trust a wolf disguised as a sheep is stupidity; to love a wolf is to yield one's heart to evil. And the warning with which our Lord introduces the adage about tree and fruit needs heeding again. We are not threatened with penalty if we act foolishly or wickedly; we are promised consequences. Man's capacities are his endowment; unlike the order of nature his fruit is a matter of his own choosing. But once he has chosen, his fruit will identify him from what he wants to be. There is visited on him the result of his own choice. "Till the end of time," said George Bernard Shaw, "hate will breed hate, murder will breed murder, war will breed war till the gods create a race that will understand." Understand what? That grapes cannot be gathered from thorns and that a man's fruit is the definitive identification of his tree.

11

The ageless problem of bringing affirmation and action into a coalition that no circumstance can disjoin is the reason for what is generally regarded as the concluding and in some ways the summarizing section of this study. His listeners had presumably assented to much that he had said. Certainly the proverbs which represented for them the solid common sense that he had distilled from life would have evoked their hearty response: "Lord, Lord." This audience reaction, as we call it, is manifest in the types of applause we give to what elicits our satisfaction. "You said it!" shouts one; "You can say that again!" shouts another. In more decorous congregations it will take the form of the tired post-service comment about how much the sermon was enjoyed.

But compliment does not take the place of commitment. Hence Jesus predicts, "Not every one who says to me, 'Lord, Lord,' shall enter the kingdom of heaven, but he who does the will of my Father who is in heaven" (Matt. 7:21). This, he goes on to say, will occasion vast surprise; for those who were most confident of their credentials for entrance into the kingdom will discover not only that they are valueless but that they who present them are evildoers. Even those who could boast that they had used his name in the doing of "mighty works," in prophesying and exorcising demons, are dismissed for what one thinks deserves reward; it is something else to be told one is a stranger to the object of his alleged devotion. He who had never known the Father found at last that the nonrecognition was mutual.

This is hard doctrine, but the problem to which it is addressed is hard. It states simply that if man opts the will of God, he must practice it. Not perfectly but with single-minded devotion. No incantation, the intonation of no sacred name, no pretension, however pious or persistent, can be substituted for the doing of the Father's will. Indeed, the wiles of the hypocrite, who is the most versatile user of names and histrionics for impressing his audience, ultimately deceive no one; and he finally moves from the intersection where he has stood, trumpet in hand, or head bowed in ostentatious devotions, or disheveled and pitiful, expelled as a doer of evil.

At this point proverb gives place to parable; and though it is not easy to select his most familiar, certainly the little story about the two men and their houses and the buffeting storms is as ingratiating as any he spoke. But this parable partakes of the nature of proverb in that it is monitory rather than mandatory. Life comes to all men alike; they are confronted by it and must, as best they can, accomodate themselves to it. This is not easy; security is never absolute, and man, while he seeks it, must protect himself against the illusion of absolute safety and perfect contentment. As George F. Kennan put it, we need "those real underpinnings of existence, founded in faith, modesty, humor, and a sense of relativity, on which alone a tolerable human existence can be built." [3]

Set opposite each other in this parable we do not find the honest man and the hypocrite; we find the wise man and the fool. They are caught in the same necessity—building a house—they suffer the same weather—the rain, the floods, and the beating wind. One survives; the other is lost in the mighty crash of his house. And while we affirm the sturdy good sense of the man who built on a rock, we are less inclined to condemn than to pity the fool who thought that sand was good enough for the kind of house he was building.

Comment on this familiar passage has been voluminous, and there is no necessity for adding to it here. Pertinent to

---

[3] "The Illusion of Security," *The Atlantic Monthly*, Aug., 1954, p. 34.

our inquiry into what Jesus saw in man is the observation that he is destroyed as often by his folly as by his unrighteousness. Conversely, he is saved by his wisdom as often as by his integrity. Once again let us be careful not to build too commodious a structure on this fact. It does not follow that all a man needs for security is wisdom or that a sinner is just a fool caught in his stupidity. We will do better if, as Kennan says, we have faith, modesty, and humor and a sense of relativity as foundation for the structure of our lives. And we must remember what we have just been told, that it is the man who does the will of the Father who enters the kingdom of heaven, not the man who simply flees folly and pursues wisdom. To build a house that will not collapse requires all man's ingenuity and devotion to the basic principles of right construction. Even then cracks may appear in the walls and water seep into the basement. But man has a chance to exercise his judgment. His house may shatter even though he has built it well; but if it falls, it will not be because in the nature of things man cannot build wisely.

"And when Jesus finished these sayings, the crowds were astonished at his teaching, for he taught them as one who had authority, and not as their scribes." (Matt. 7:28-29.) What authoirty? The law, the prophets, and common sense!

CHAPTER VIII

Man in Society

Our study of the proverbs of Jesus has enabled us to see something of that area of human experience that lies outside the jurisdictions of law and prophecy, or, as I have put it, law and religion. It is the area of option rather than obligation. Distilled wisdom, or common sense, has something to say about many of the predicaments into which man stumbles, in the hope that he will profit by it. If he doesn't, he is not culpable in terms of law; he is commiserable in terms of a practical concensus shared by many of his fellows. Some of the most pungent of Jesus' proverbs have not been considered here. For example: "Every one who exalts himself will be humbled, and he who humbles himself will be exalted" (Luke 14:11); "he who finds his life will lose it, and he who loses his life for my sake will find it" (Matt. 10:39). Others come readily to mind; and they illustrate still further how wisely Jesus dealt with that enormous area of human experience that cannot be subsumed under moral, legal, or religious categories.

This is the area within which compromise, improvisation, and the relativity of balanced action are often necessary. The perfect is the enemy of the good, says a French maxim. When Jesus confronted the illusion of perfect security, he advised that those treasures that invite the maximum risk be discarded for those that involve a minimum threat. This, as has been said, is misunderstood if it is regarded as a law demanding improvidence. It is common sense, and we can accept it or not as we will. Such latitude of choice is not allowed in dealing with the moral absolutes: murder, adultery, honesty, and the like. We agree that killing is too grave a matter to be settled with a proverb; and when we treat it as a matter concerning which we can make compromises or accommodations, we lose something far more irrecoverable than we lose to moths, rust, and thieves. It is never easy to draw the margins that separate moral law and common sense, but it is the moral responsibility of those who confront life seriously to do so. The differences, in other words, between folly and sin, between cleverness and rectitude, are easily blurred. This is the point of the famous remark attributed to Talleyrand: "It is worse than a crime—it is a blunder." We may not be as confident as he was, but we must try.

1

Up to this point this study has led us to the consideration of those qualities of the heart of man to which Jesus addressed himself in his fulfillment of law and prophecy and in his proverbs. But within the body of the material under review we have encountered half a dozen times a phrase: the kingdom of heaven. It is not proposed that a study of this freighted phrase engage us here. The concern is that it may be used to expose from another angle what Jesus thought of man. He saw him as an individual, but he knew that what he was was significantly affected by his relations within the society he shared, and that what he was could and did affect that society.

Why the idea of the community of those dedicated to life as Jesus proclaimed it—those who accepted the Good News—is alternately called the kingdom of God and the kingdom of heaven is a matter for discussion by specialists. Matthew uses mainly the latter; Luke and Mark prefer the former. The Fourth Gospel uses the kingdom of God twice, the other phrase not at all. And while there is much that Mark calls the "mystery of the kingdom," there is one emphasis that Matthew supplies that we regard as both clear and important. As he records the parables of the kingdom, he represents Jesus as giving man an initiative in its affairs that is not found in the other Gospels. If this, as some suggest, is due to Jewish influence in the formative years of the new community, it would not seem for that reason to reflect any less clearly a concept that was in the mind of Jesus.

At once the series of seven vignettes in the thirteenth chapter of Matthew comes to mind. He is presented as confronting such a crowd that he had to get into a boat. He sat down and "told them many things in parables." And by way of introduction he says: "Truly, I say to you, many prophets and righteous men longed to see what you see, and did not see it, and to hear what you hear, and did not hear it" (Matt. 13:17). What was this new thing? Prophets, many of them, and other righteous men had down the centuries heard about a kingdom, always referred to as *the* kingdom, *his* kingdom, *my* kingdom, *thy* kingdom. Was Jesus fitting a new pronoun to it? We think he was. It was *your* kingdom.

This is not a contraction of the concept of God's eternal domain to the puny dimensions of a kingdom of man. That it has been so misconceived is doubtless the result of pride, of man's lust to usurp the dominion. It is on the contrary an expansion of the great idea: in the coming of the kingdom man was not to be conscripted as a subject; he was to be enlisted as a volunteer.

Observe how this emerges from a quick reading of these parables. A sower goes out to sow the seed of the Good News, and *men* who hear it react variously and for various reasons; a good *man* sows good seed in his field but discovers that his enemy has come while he was asleep and sowed weeds. A *man* took a grain of mustard seed and sowed it in his field; a *woman* hid leaven in three measures of meal; a *man* found a treasure hidden in his field; a *merchant* went in search of fine pearls. The seventh parable, in a striking fashion to which I shall return for further comment, indicates an initiative taken by unidentified persons who throw the net of the kingdom into the sea.

The point here is that so encompassing and dominant a purpose as is caught in the phrase "the kingdom of heaven" is more than God's affair. Man's industry, faith, dutifulness, good fortune, and his dreams are all volunteered in the search he makes for the fellowship of those who hear and appropriate the Good News. Conversely also, it is sometimes what looks like bad luck—the caprice of scattered seeds— that is his undoing. These all deserve somewhat more detailed comment.

2

While there is a good deal to be said about the concept of the kingdom from the Godward side, it is clear that here we have a concern to set man within its context. These seven parables deal primarily with people. Perhaps those who first heard them spoken were already sufficiently conversant with the basic ideas of the kingdom to make unnecessary a fuller statement at that time. Indeed, it is a credible assumption that they were so accustomed to the phrase "the kingdom of God" that they had skimped their own responsibility in the enterprise. It was necessary, therefore, to remind them that God's kingdom was also the kingdom of those who were God's partisans or, to put it more simply, those who were the sons of the Father. It was the kingdom *of* heaven, not *in* heaven or *from* heaven.

The parable of the sower is a parable of both a sower and hearers, and it is the latter that get most attention. The Word of the kingdom is the seed. This was the Good News, and we cannot be mistaken if this means to us all that Jesus had been telling the multitudes who followed him. Its acceptability was to be assessed by every hearer. To the indifferent the gospel was unimportant; to the superficial it was sometimes useful, sometimes not; to the anxious and ambitious it was sterile for their purposes; and to the understanding it was fruitful in ratio to the measure of their comprehension and practice.

This is clearly a quickly sketched picture about people, and it says a good deal to us about what Jesus saw in man. The lines of the picture are bare of sentimentality; they are sharply, almost starkly realistic. It would be difficult to set down more clearly the categories into which men seem to fall unless one added the willfully and incorrigibly perverse. Was Jesus' omission of this familiar type an oversight? We do not think so, though if we were writing the parable, we would perhaps want to include it. It would be the hearer who, knowing the value of the seed, caught it as it fell, only to crush it and scatter it as dust lest it find an inch of good soil and germinate. The nearest Jesus came to this was the enemy who sowed weeds among the wheat, but that is a different matter.

In our times we have seen monsters of malevolence who have made the earth tremble under their stamping feet. They, we say, are irredeemably corrupt. There is no soil in them that can receive and nurture any good seed. This judgment is easily spread to cover all mankind. There but for the grace of God go we all. So just as we believe the grace of God can cope with every man's rebellion, we tend to regard every man as the same sort of rebel, not through his obstinacy or blindness but through his chromosomes.

But Jesus lived in the time of a Caesar who strode the world like a Colossus, and his friend and precursor John had died at the tipsy whim of a lecherous kinglet, and he himself was to be executed by the combined anger of religious and political scoundrels. He could not have been indifferent to such; was he then placing them outside the reach of the

Good News, or did he include them in the four classes to whom the good seed was scattered? We do not know.

Nevertheless what was true in his time, as he looked at man and the gospel, is unchanged in our time. The "path" on which the indifferent or preoccupied hurry today is smooth with centuries of traffic, and where we are headed or what we are doing is so engrossing that the seed falls and we do not understand it and it is snatched away. The Good News is to us sentimentality, dream; it is the lovely but insubstantial hope of a first-century romantic who knew more about birds and lilies than about men. "This is what was sown along the path" (Matt. 13:19.) However, not all hurry along, impatient with dreams. Instead of a smooth path the way may be rocky. Life, that is to say, is rough; it is hard going. Any reassuring word, any good news, any fantasy, will beguile for a while. This hearer thinks he has a promising formula for good fortune; now at last he can get out of the rocks and rubble. But life is never to be smooth for him; he must learn to live amidst its rigors, its "tribulation or persecution," and its defeats. Only as he has a root in himself (here the figure is mixed but no matter) will the Good News germinate and produce results. Otherwise "immediately he falls away" (Matt. 13:21).

Nor do we all stumble in rocky ground. The smooth path or the rough one may give place to more spacious areas. Here there is not so much of difficulty as there is of delight. The "cares of the world" may, of course, be understood as anxieties; but more plainly they may be the things we care about. And that would mean the things we value, or love, or spend ourselves for. The "delight in riches"—we know what that means whether it is as munificent as a small boy's dime for an ice-cream cone or as meager as an insatiable coupon clipper's stock certificates. The trouble here, obviously, is the illusion of security, the spurious confidence that palpable values are permanent values. The good news that says security is no illusion if it rests in impalpable values is old hat; it has been what the impoverished dreamers have always prated about! It is their defense against the suspicion of indigency. Thus the word is choked, and "it proves unfruitful" (Matt. 13:22).

And finally there is the good ground: the smooth, fecund, tended soil that is the seed plot of hearing and understanding and action. These folk may once have hurried impatiently along the hard path or stumbled across the stony field or dallied with the delights of the "world." They are not in another world; their world—or their ground—has been cultivated so that in varying degrees they hear and understand and accept the good news of the kingdom and bear its fruit for the harvesting of others, "in one case a hundredfold, in another sixty, and in another thirty" (Matt. 13:23).

3

There are two extremes at which the hope of society is threatened by disillusionment. Some say people are so bad that no social structure can survive human selfishness. The tombstones of dead cultures all bear the same somber epitaph: suicide. This may be the judgment of realism; it is also the saturnine confession of cynicism. The other extreme gaily says that people are all so good that not only is the perfect society possible; it is here. To be sure, this sounds like idiocy; but its pluck and amiability are ingratiating.

How is it possible to escape the sober pessimism of the realist and the silly optimism of the utopian? If the latter loses himself in illusion, the former immobilizes himself in his despair. Now of one thing we may be certain: Jesus was neither cynic nor utopian. He knew what was in man, and this saved him from the extremes of defeatism and escapism. It is to this situation that the second parable speaks.

A man, so the story goes, "sowed good seed in his field" (Matt. 13:24). The soil, we may assume had been prepared and the grain carefully scattered. But while he was sleeping, an enemy came and sowed weeds which in due time sprouted amid the early blades of wheat. It was apparent that the crop was threatened. What to do? His men proposed to root out the weeds, but the owner demurred. "No," he said; "lest in gathering the weeds you root up the wheat along with them. Let both grow together until the harvest; and at harvest time I will tell the reapers, Gather the weeds first and bind them in bundles to be burned, but gather the wheat into my barn." (13:29-30.)

This, we submit, is a confrontation of the problem of society that escapes the cynic's certainty that all men are weeds and the utopian's illusion that all men are wheat. "The good seed means the sons of the kingdom; the weeds are the sons of the evil one." (13:38.) We are not concerned here with origins and genetics; what is important to us is first, the discovery that Jesus saw that men, good and bad, would have to live together; and second, that there was an ultimate judgment to be rendered on society when its evil and good would finally be separated.

It is perhaps easier for us to accept the first proposition than the second. Certainly we see the weeds and the wheat growing together though we will most likely describe the "sons of the evil one" in more mordant terms than weeds or tares. It is the fact of ultimate judgment that we aren't sure of. It seems unduly put off; have not the weeds already threatened sufficiently the life of the wheat? How much longer can we endure slow strangulation by the fast-growing evils of the world?

So the illusionists press the ultimate day of judgment out beyond an eschatological sunset when in an apocalypse of flame the holocaust of burning weeds will light the sky.

And the cynics who are too myopic to see beyond history predict that the field ("the field is the world") is already doomed, not only to a worthless yield of wheat but to a suffocating luxuriance of weeds. Is the attitude of Jesus as he exhibited it in the little story more honest with the facts of society even as they are observed by us today? I think it is and for the reason that he saw more clearly than the cynic and the utopian. "He who has ears, let him hear." (13:43.)

4

"The smallest of all seeds, . . . when it has grown it is the greatest of shrubs and becomes a tree, so that the birds of the air come and make nests in its branches." (Matt. 13:32.) If there was need to step in between the cynic and the utopian and find a realistic place for the kingdom of heaven, it was also necessary to reassure the fainthearted that origins do not determine values. This is an answer to what philosophers call the genetic fallacy: "the depreciatory appraisal of the product of a historical or evolutionary process because of its lowly origin."

No matter that we know seeds smaller and shrubs larger than mustard although we are told that in Palestine the herb did grow fifteen feet tall. The point of this is simple: there is in the kingdom idea a vital social principle that can grow to phenomenal dimensions. Beyond this, however, is the necessity that the faith and the initiative of individuals must take the seed and plant it.

There is reason for thinking that it was necessary to say this to Jesus' friends. They were surrounded by the limitless horizons of the Roman world, and the might of the giant imperium dwarfed to microscopic puniness the pretensions of sowers who said the "field is the world." This was not a seditious movement; it was a preposterous folly deserving laughter rather than fear. Even those who yearned for freedom from the imperial yoke could see little hope in this group of Galilean peasants. Bolder and more ruthless men than they had been crushed like vermin under the heels of legionaries. What then was this tiny seed to sprout? Green ephemera to live through the night and wither under the day's bland radiance?

Not so, said Jesus, but a stout and hospitable tree, the haven of nesting birds and the bearer of pungent seed to be used as condiment or medicine. But this seed, though it might grow wild in the uncultivated wastelands, must be planted in the fields, and planted in faith that within its wee diameters was a stirring, insurgent vitality that, given a chance to grow, would tower beyond the reach of a man's hand or even his hope. It was something to have such a responsibility put in one's hand. Would man have been trusted with a mustard seed if both he and it had not deserved it?

5

"The kingdom of heaven is like leaven." (Matt. 13:33.) It is hard to overstate the importance of this. For generations the people of Israel had been nurtured in the hope of cataclysm. It was the dramatic that revealed the purposes and power of God. A destroying army was his avenger; three years of dewless and rainless suffering were a divine judgment against the iniquities of Ahab and Jezebel; "the fingers of a man's hand appeared and wrote on the plaster of the wall of the king's palace" (Dan. 5:5), and Belshazzar palsied in the presence of the scribbled sentence of death.

To be sure, there were voices that spoke of long-suffering patience that intercepted the falling doom because God was merciful and of great compassion; but by the measure that makes the theatrical more evocative than the prosaic, men tended to think of the divine activity as more violent than gradual. The Eternal rode on the wings of the wind; he made the storms his messengers and flame and fire his ministers (Ps. 104:3-4).

It has never been easy to be patient, for patience is a state of mind that is stoutly resistant to the impulse to precipitate or radical action. Otherwise it is simple flaccidity or indifference. Therefore the Son of man coming as a thief in the night, and the new Jerusalem descending as a radiant gem-studded giant cube from the sky, and Satan catapulted at last in one final plunge into the lake of fire—these all indicated after a fashion the impatience of God, a necessity pressed upon him by the wickedness of the sons of earth. Present-day fondness for eschatology is correlative to a renewed conviction of the depth and pervasiveness of man's sin. Human resources of heart and mind seem so perversely unable to resist the rising tides of cruelty and hatred that we look with hope toward the rending of the sky and the coming of deliverance on the clouds of heaven.

We must not lose sight of this; it is a mood of the spirit, and every such mood is authentic as long as it lasts. Nevertheless it must not be allowed to shut off our view of the leaven hidden in three measures of meal. In the story of the mustard seed that achieved unpredictable size we have one aspect of growth. In the leaven we have another; here the point is not size, it is permeation. And this is important because size in itself can be deceptive; it is what is inside that makes the difference.

Furthermore for some reason Jesus describes the woman's action as *hiding* the leaven. This is either a careless use of a word or deliberate. There is surely nothing furtive in her act; it is not concealment on which she is determined, for once the meal was leavened, the secret could not be kept. No; the suggestion would rather seem to be less that the woman was hiding something than that the ingredient she was adding seemed so unobtrusive. Under a microscope the fission of a yeast cell may be called dramatic, but in a mass of dough it is so gradual as to be inconspicuous. And yet in terms of its power and permeation yeast is one of nature's prodigies.

The temptation to moralize this little parable has rarely been successfully resisted by those who have reflected on it. The air is full of yeast spores ready to fall on any moist substance containing sugar and begin their rapid germination. A yeast cell when full-grown puts out buds, and chains or clusters of the tiny one-celled plants are formed. Then they break apart and form new colonies while the cell walls rupture, scattering their microscopic spores on the wind to find new hosts and to begin again the busy cycle of cell, colony, division, and dispersion. This (Jesus' use of yeast as a simile for the kingdom of heaven) we would like to think is an amazing exhibition of scientific prescience fifteen centuries before Galileo invented the microscope. Since this could not have been the case, the intention of the parable must be found not so much in the method of the diffusive power of the kingdom but in the initiative of the anonymous housewife who was busy about her chores. She was a woman of diligence and hope; she was not slack in her preparation, and she believed *all* the meal would be leavened.

As has often been said, this sort of story was something Jesus' hearers could understand. They did not know about spores, gametes, germination, ferment, and such things and processes; but they knew what happened when good yeast was mixed into good meal. As pious folk do, they would have assigned the mystery to the doings of their Father in heaven; but for all that they would not have expected him to appear in the kitchen to mix the ingredients and set the loaf after the magic of swelling was performed. If the baked loaf was to be put on the table, the woman had to prepare it; if the kingdom of heaven was to come, its yeasty power would have to be infused into the lump of the world's life by those who were committed to its leavening. The initiative was man's; the ingerminating power was God's.

6

"The kingdom of heaven is like treasure hidden in a field." (Matt. 13:44.) There are intimations in this simile that are mildly disturbing. We have been told that in times when a man could not trust his treasure to a safety-deposit box, he dug a hole and stashed it away. So when we see this man cutting across a field and stumbling over a treasure chest, we are disappointed that he did not seek out the owner of either the cache or the field and report his find. When, instead, he kicked dirt over the strongbox and hurried off to talk to his broker, he looked suspiciously like a dishonest person.

These are not matters to quibble over; obviously if the owner of the treasure was also the owner of the field, his selling field and treasure together was his own affair. If the treasure had been hidden by a trespasser, perhaps his trespass was justly rewarded by the loss. If, furthermore, the buyer saw values in the field that its owner knew nothing about, there was no culpability involved in either buying or selling.

This, however, would seem to be quite beside the point. What Jesus was doing was clearly reminding his friends that the values of the kingdom—and it is interesting that at this point he has turned from the kingdom energies of growth and penetration to its *value* aspects—are neither remote nor obvious. "The field is the world," and these values are underfoot, so to speak; but they are found only by those who have sharp eyes, and they are to be had only by those who are willing to exchange all they have in order to possess them.

Here again we think he was bending their attention away

from a preoccupation that was widely current, one that persists, indeed, at the present. Engrossed as we all are with things that are a part of the customary furnishings and routine operations of daily living, we easily slip into the mistake of thinking that the values of the kingdom are somewhere else and, perhaps, in the possession of a select clientele who have been exempt from ordinary living. Thus the values of a community or a fellowship of the partisans of God are *out there somewhere* and to be had *over there sometime*. Until such a change of our fortunes comes about, we will grub in our thriveless fields in the hope not of finding treasure but of eking out an existence.

Now while this is a common atttude, the rebuke to it is almost as common. Not only did Jesus tell a parable about a man who found values right underfoot; nearly every lore has the same story in one form or another. The search for the bluebird of happiness ends in finding the bluebird in one's own back yard. Indeed, the kingdom of heaven was not far from a rich young ruler who was looking for it; it was already within others who had not realized it. And the point that this parable of a universal observation on human experience was making was that what we need for the kingdom is not remote or difficult; it is at hand. At the same time it is dear, not to be had for the mere picking up but paid for with all that one can raise for the bargain.

Again we need to be reminded that this was strange talk to people who were hedged and hectored by overlords who took from them most of their meager holdings. In such straitened circumstances it was easy to despair, or to defer their hope, to dream of treasure hidden in an *eschaton*. And yet all about them was the kingdom's wealth. It was not in fields or secret hoardings; it was in human individuals with all their richness of companionship and caring. When our Lord set forth on his kingdom enterprise, he found treasure by the seaside in fishing boats, at the tax taker's bench, yes, and on the rooftop of the house of a member of the Sanhedrin. And he gave all that he had that he might possess it.

7

Here is another value reference to the kingdom of heaven. "The kingdom of heaven is like a merchant in search of fine pearls, who, on finding one pearl of great value, went and sold all that he had and bought it." (Matt. 13:45.) This time we do not see a man stumbling on a treasure-trove; we see a man in a tireless and finally rewarded search. Nor is this to be conducted in a field; he roves the world over looking for the "one pearl of great value."

This introduces a quality of the human spirit that exerts a strong sentimental pull on all of us. It is the invincible dream in the heart that drives and restrains, illumines or confuses, but will not desist or die.

He whom a dream hath possessed knoweth no more of roaming;
All roads and the flowing of waves and the speediest flight he
    knows,
But wherever his feet are set, his soul is forever homing,
And going, he comes, and coming he heareth a call and goes.[1]

What was it in the heart of a beekeeper in New Zealand that compelled him to set forth on a journey that ended after weeks of punishing and perilous assault in fifteen aching minutes on the pinnacle of the earth's frozen apex? "Why do Alpinists climb mountains?" "Because they are there," was the answer. But this is the modest reply of courage. It

---

[1] "He Whom a Dream Hath Possessed." From *Jealous of Dead Leaves* by Shaemas O'Sheel, Copyright R 1955 Annette K. O'Sheel, by permission of Liveright Publishers, New York.

is the mountain's forbidding summit in the heart that demands ascent. But why that?

What was it in the heart of a medical student in London that induced him to go through months of acute physical torture in a training program that produced alternate shock and blackout and quick recovery and action? To break the four-minute mile, said young Roger Bannister. But why that?

There is no accounting for the dream in the heart. Even those who pursue it most relentlessly cannot explain it. And those in whom it seems to have died are surprised and intrigued by the recurring mystery of its resurrection. There are some who tell us that when the "insubstantial fragment" is lost, there is still left the dream of the dream. "Thou hast made me hope" (Ps. 119:49), said the ancient poet, which is little different from being made to dream. If man is made to dream, when he ceases to dream, he ceases to be.

The merchant in our story tells us this. A connoisseur of fine gems he must many times have held them in caressing fingers noting their satin iridescence in the soft light. And still he had not yet felt the finest. All the loveliness he had known was but an invitation to further search. There was one perfect pearl in his heart that some day would be in his hand.

I have said that this parable exerts a sentimental pull on all our hearts. Perhaps this should be resisted in the name of realism. Was not this merchant nothing more than a merchant, the pearl he wanted nothing more than a business investment? It is agreed that much of the feverish questing of our times is little more than this, and being practical people we incline to smile indulgently at explanations that disguise our frenzy with fancy. But Jesus was not the sort of observer of life who promises a pot of gold at the rainbow's end. He was far too much of a realist for that. It is not the language of sentimentalism that says he too had a dream in his heart. We call it purpose, or will, or doing something. It is redemption, or salvation, or reconcilation. But it is not less a dream, a pearl of great price. We even say he paid for it by the anguish of the cross, and some have said that his expiring cry "It is finished" meant that this pearl of great price had been finally won.

Such comments are legitimate though they lead us into the speculations of theology. He was hardly talking to his hearers in such a vein. Pearl merchants they had seen in market and bazaar and envied them as they watched the cool *nacré* roundness of their wares slip through the fingers that displayed them to possible buyers, Jesus himself had seen them and admired their loveliness and the fondness with which they were exhibited. And he knew that it is part of the heart's function to dream of better gems, of the best and ultimate jewel, and that once the vision is seen and the quest begun, man has given demonstration of the intimation of God in his soul.

Sentimental? The answer is partially that there is an impressive record of searchers who with the kingdom of heaven in their hearts have pursued it down the years and across the earth. We call them saints and heroes perhaps; we rarely call them sentimentalists: Socrates and the free mind, Luther and an unfettered faith, Roger Williams and a free society, Wilberforce and a slaveless world, Lincoln and a more perfect union. And if in our proudly practical age we have set our hearts on values more immediately useful than gems, it may rebuke us as we appraise the worth of what our pursuit has won for us. Of course a man may dream of evil as well as of good. We call this sin; but let us not dismiss as mawkish the capacity to dream and to pursue, and let us take care lest because some pearl of great price has eluded us, we cast our lesser pearls before swine.

8

"Again, the kingdom of heaven is like a net which was thrown into the sea and gathered fish of every kind." (Matt. 13:47.) In some respects this is the most interesting of the parables. Here there is human initiative again; but it is men this time, not a single individual. At least it was men who drew the net ashore, and we assume a collective initiative in its casting. The sea is a more spacious area than the field where seed was sown and treasure found; and the principle of social selectivity in terms of utility, sorting the good into vessels and throwing away the bad, is an insight that startles us with its contemporaneity and practicality.

The emphasis cannot be missed: men cast the net; the net catches the fish. If we stop long enough to observe the operation, the idea it suggests is very vivid. The combined efforts of men practical in their craft throw the net in a wide circumference over the surface of water that both contains and conceals its hoard of fish. As it settles out of sight, there is no predicting what and how much luck will recompense the effort. But the disappointment of a meager haul will not daunt the fisherman. Better luck next time; the law of averages will sustain his hope. He will stop neither today because he caught nothing nor tomorrow because he caught more than he could pull ashore.

This simile was of course familiar; but its full import—if it was appreciated—was startling. The idea of the kingdom of heaven had been for the most part an exclusive concept. To be sure, there were occasional visionaries who talked of Mount Zion as the ultimate gathering place of all the nations, but this was not put in the form of a net enclosing them so much as a compulsion drawing them. There was fierce resentment against Roman efforts to assimilate the

Jews into its alien culture, and those who were caught in its net were renegades, unfilial sons of Abraham.

To say, then, that the kingdom of heaven was abandoning exclusivism for the inclusion of wider values of the surrounding cultural sea was a notion that had long been resisted. Was it a subtle imitation of Rome? Or was it not rather a recognition of the nature of dynamic society and a provision for it in the new movement of the Good News?

To be sure, society is a fiction; only the individuals who compose it are real. The net—which I think here symbolizes society—was real enough; but it took men to use it. Nevertheless it is true—Is it not?—that the activity of individuals in the aggregate has the appearance of reality. We are not fooling ourselves when we talk of society or culture as though it has initiative or activity that seems independent of one's individual behavior. It is necessary always to recognize the tension between the group and the individual and to use it creatively. We cannot as individuals escape into isolation any more than we can succumb to denaturing at the hands of society. Part of the world's present confusion centers about the question as to how far one is to suffer defacement by the leviathan state or suffer desication by an unattenuated individualism.

With these circumstances in mind we are able to see what a striking principle Jesus suggested in the seventh parable. There are two tendencies in a vital society; the first is the creative-conservative. Out of such indigenous resources as are found within itself, it develops and consolidates and protects its life. The second is the appropriative-assimilative. Out of such exogenous resources as are found in neighbor cultures, values are appropriated and assimilated insofar as they promise to enhance viability. Neither of these processes can be suppressed or discarded. To isolate one's society from external influences is to suffer the degenerative effects of inbreeding, spiritual as well as physical; to abandon the pattern of one's culture in the enthusiasm for accepting another is to suffer the demoralizing effects of indecision, impermanence, and social opportunism.

The dialectic between these two forces is manifest in almost every area of modern life, but that it was implicit in the idea of the kingdom as Jesus pictured it in the simile of the net is insufficiently realized. The tendency of the religious society or community or culture is predominantly conservative. It develops dogma to protect itself from the invasion of alien ideas and creates institutions and priest sentinels to warn against marauders and reassure the beleaguered. Conversely, the tendency of so-called secular society is more generally adventurous. Its values are more frankly practical or material, and it will risk much of its own wealth if it thinks the wealth of other societies can be appropriated and assimilated. Ironically each tendency creates hostility, and there is little to choose between the wars of religion waged in the defense of conservatism and the wars of secular cultures fought for continents and markets. There is much to support the idea that if we are to be spared cosmic destruction in a final Armageddon, we shall have to admit and accept as essential to group (national, cultural) life both of these dynamic social energies. What that can do for our present tortured world life, it is not difficult to foresee. That culture is most mature and most stable that has learned to live within this dialectic tension.

Now historically, whether our Lord was predicting it or not, this is what happened to the kingdom of heaven, or as we may prefer to call it, the Christian movement. The story of the way in which ideas, organization, and ritual were appropriated by the Church in its first four centuries of contact with an alien world has been endlessly told. There is considerable dismay in some quarters at the continual and growing evidence that what we see in the contemporary world is not the simple Galilean fellowship or its uncomplicated and lucid testimony. And those who claim for themselves that they preserve and practice the uncorrupted pattern of New Testament order and witness are unaware of either the rudimentary dynamics of society or the plain facts of history. The net has been widely cast into undimensioned seas of thought and action. Christian churches in the Orient have been built to look like temples. Shocking? But what was the architectural prototype of the Gothic cathedral? Certainly not a synagogue in Nazareth.

Indeed, this net casting has been the impetus behind the missionary expansion of Christendom; and if that has "gathered fish of every kind," that is exactly what was previsioned in the parable. And when the fellowship began in Jerusalem and went forth into Judea and Samaria, and to the uttermost parts of the earth, there had begun the most prodigious net casting the world has ever seen.

This is not to say that the Christian movement has been all-inclusive or undiscriminating. On the contrary; part of the churning seascape we have been looking at shows us men, after they have pulled in the net, sorting the catch and separating the good from the bad. They knew their craft: certain varieties of fish were edible and would find a market; certain others were good-for-nothing. They were judged on the basis of their utility; the merely ornamental was as sure a discard as the inedible.

Here we see what we are accustomed to call the principle of judgment that rests over the total human enterprise. As individuals we stand beneath it; as societies and cultures we cannot escape it. Perhaps we think too superficially of judgment in terms of utility; God, we have reasons for thinking, has criteria more profound than simple usefulness or the values that accrue only to human advantage. It is man's sin rather than his inutility that is an offense to God; and as this little parable closes—"so it will be at the close of the age" —we get a vivid picture of just how deep the offense is and how condign its punishment.

9

To think that the optimism of Jesus could project so important a future for the partisans of God is to realize the measure of confidence he had in his friends. That they had confidence in themselves is shown in the conclusion of the episode within which these parables were told. " 'Have you understood all this?' They said to him, 'Yes.' " It must have been an encouraging reply; we wonder if it was mere politeness or solid conviction. Lest it be the former, he went on to give a final emphasis to his confidence in them. "And he said to them, 'Therefore every scribe who has been trained for the kingdom of heaven is like a householder who brings out of his treasure what is new and what is old.' " (Matt. 13:52.) There's the note again: the new and the old. But the ability to fetch the new and the old is not the result of cleverness or endowment; it is the competence of those who are trained for the kingdom of heaven. Perhaps some of our difficulty is that we think the amateur is more proficient than the trained scribe. But it is the amateur who has most difficulty distinguishing the novel—and its hopes—from the old —and its established values. And it is the amateur whose fears throw him into dangerous conservatism. What is it that the trained scribe knows? Perhaps we may find a simple answer to that.

CHAPTER IX

The New and the Old

As Matthew continues the record, Jesus is seen at home again in the town of Nazareth, standing as a teacher in the synagogue. The response he won from his hearers was curiously mixed: they conceded that he spoke wisdom, they wondered where he had acquired it, and they were scandalized in him *(skandalizo en auto)*. Perhaps our word "scandal" has a sharper edge than its early Greek equivalent, but not much. "Offended" is the more common rendering, "caused to stumble" an even gentler term. However mildly we may translate it, the effect reported is surprising. Why should wisdom be scandalous? That's a good question! Or more correctly, why should one who speaks wisdom be offensive or an occasion of stumbling? That's another good question.

It is interesting to note that the response Jesus made to their surprise and affront was apparently free from pique. He might have pointed out that they put themselves in an impossible position in respect to wisdom, but he didn't. Rather, he said that the prophet is in an impossible position. He "is not without honor except in his own country and in his own house" (Matt. 13:57). Nevertheless it was the people who suffered the final penalty, not the prophet, who "did not do many mighty works there, because of their unbelief" (13:58). We are not told what it was they did not believe in —whether him or what he said.

1

Now there is a possibility that the reason for the sense of shock he induced was that wisdom is both old and new. This is another way of saying that it is neither old nor new; it is ageless. We are not quite sure of this, so the antiquarian who values wisdom because it is old is suspicious of the contemporary who values wisdom because of its novelty. We need to be reminded that it was in the language of Jesus the same storehouse out of which new and old things were brought by the well-trained scribe.

It is surely faint praise to award to Jesus the rating of a well-trained scribe, but there can be no dispute about the fact. It has been often pointed out that there is nothing in the teachings of Jesus that is not either explicit or implicit in the stored wisdom of his people. Thus it was old. The novelty or freshness which arrests us and scandalized his hearers lies in the way he put things together. This is, I believe, most engagingly illustrated in his reply to the question as to what was the first and greatest commandment. He went back into the storehouse and fetched the great and sonorous words of Deut. 6:5: "You shall love the Lord your God with all your heart, and with all your soul, and with all your might." This was ancient enough and great enough. A parallel commandment was also brought from the same storehouse: Lev. 19:18: "'You shall not take vengeance or bear any grudge against the sons of your own people, *but* you shall love your neighbor as yourself." The adversative conjunction is important. The correct attitude toward one's own people is negatively stated: no vengeance, no grudge; the attitude toward one's neighbor (not one's own people) is positively stated in terms of love. This too was old, but novelty lay in the fact that he characterized it not as different from one's love for God but as similar to it. What had once been regarded as two mandates were merged into one. Identification of the two is suggested at several points in the apocryphal book the Testaments of the Twelve Patriarchs; but how widely this had been accepted by the time of Jesus, it is impossible to know. The measure of this novelty is found in the fact that today we, as the ancients for the most part, regard them as two commands; and if we are not careful in our understanding of them, they turn out, unhappily, to be not identical but opposites. Love God? Yes. Love man? Impossible.

Impossible only if we misconceive the meaning of love. It has nothing to do with the romantic sentiment which, however profound and creative in human experience it would appear, if applied to God's love for us or our's for him, would be shallow to the point almost of frivolousness. Nor does it mean the familial, domestic, or wider social expressions of human mutuality. Romantic love seeks to possess the object of its concern; domestic love seeks to protect rather than possess. Each is necessary for human survival, but neither is appropriate as a description of God's love.

Grace may come nearer as a descriptive word. It is a commonplace of Christian thought that God's love is manifest in grace. Nothing sentimental or defensive fringes this concept, for grace is the process of doing for the object on one's concern what he cannot do for himself. This effort to achieve good—the maximum good if love is one's dominant motive—stops short of nothing but perfection; it is reconciling and redeeming; it is often heroic in the truest meaning of the word. Call it the will to good, or simply good will, or—more subtly—conscience.

This is the love of God. This also is the love we must exercise toward our neighbor who may evoke in us no romantic rapture, demand no inclusion in our family or social group; but who does ask—by being our neighbor—that we give ourselves for his good—his total good. This is what even "the least" may claim because this love is in them, in us, and in God himself.

2

Deut. 6:4, the Shema, as it is known in Jewish liturgy, is today used principally as the opening of the evening service for the Sabbath and at festivals. In pious Jewish families it is repeated twice daily. The fact that it is also used as a part of Christian liturgy is a witness to its power in centering the whole of one's attention on God, the heart of the worship experience. But nothing in the Shema refers to one's neighbor. The invasion of one's total attention on God by concern for one's neighbor could very well be disruptive of the necessary concentration worship needs. The Jews were very neighbor-conscious. It is surprising to discover how carefully their neighbor contacts, both individual and group, were recognized and regulated. This is even more surprising when we remember the profound sense of exclusivism that came later to inform the Hebrew mind. By the time of Jesus it was necessary to ask who one's neighbor was.

According to the Jewish law man's primary and total allegiance was to the Lord, the one Yahweh. This was in acknowledgment of a covenant relation, but it was more than that: it was an effort to bring the total self into an attitude of devotion. Heart, in Hebrew psychology the seat of the mind, and will, and soul, not the Greek entity but the source of vitality [1] that is lost when the body dies, these three (mind, will, and soul) are commandeered with "might" in the posture of adoring dedication. However well or badly this analysis of the psyche may suit the patterns that satisfy us, it is unlikely that we shall contrive its more complete conscription than does this ancient formula. Nothing in the fortunes, good or bad, of Israel changed it. By the time of Jesus it was old but not antiquated. He seems to have believed that man had a heart that enclosed a reasoning mind and an activating will, and that both could be put under orders by the command to love God wholly. This was the first com-

---

[1] Cf. the philosophy of Henri Bergson and his metaphysics of the *élan vital* and ethics based on love as the impulse of creativity. Bergson was born a Jew and died an unbaptized convert to Roman Catholicism.

mand because it initiated man's relation to God; it was the greatest command because it left no factor of man's being outside the circumference of devotion.

3

Neighbor relations, however, would naturally seem to rest on a different level. We can be commanded to love God, but can the verb "to love" be used in the imperative mood when we confront our neighbor? The mind that yields itself to the mystery of God finds one's neighbor no mystery at all. The will, which by covenanted accord is committed to God, is not by prearrangement covenanted to one's neighbor. And the soul, which animates man's devotion to the divine, may, and very often does, activate hostility to one's neighbor.

Since man deals with two distinct entities—God and neighbor—is it not plausible to assume that a different posture of the spirit should be offered to each? Furthermore if *all* our love is conscripted for God, how is there to be any left over for neighbors? Love of God demands everything we have and are. Our neighbor, therefore, asks impiety of us if he seeks our love; and we are less than totally committed to God if we love our neighbor at all.

This created a dilemma for the Jew. His love of God, or to put it in terms less suspected of sentimentalism, the Godward orientation of his life, was the central fact of his culture. And it was this that made it difficult to get along with neighbor aliens. The Jews were a separate people; separatism is the barrier against which intercourse beats in vain. Worse than that it creates a state of man that in preserving its isolation tends to hostile attitudes toward outsiders. The problem was: How protect their cultural integrity against alien invasion and social introversion? Put in modern terms this states the difficulties we have belonging to the United Nations without eroding the granite bulwarks of our national sovereignty.

Thus the word "neighbor" becomes either a synonym for friend or a euphemism for a stranger. And if we want to be moralistic about it, we can explain that since all our love is given to God, we have none left over for our neighbor. We ought not to love him; civility is as much as can be expected, and he must deserve even that.

Now we believe that Jesus in putting these two commandments together in saying that the second is *like* the first, not a supplement to it, resolved the dilemma that we, no less than his own generation, struggle with. If in loving our neighbor we are not pinching off a fragment of the love we owe entirely to God, *we must love what is God in our neighbor.* Thus in loving God we are loving our neighbor because God is in him, and in loving our neighbor we are loving God for the same reason. What draws me to my neighbor is not his stature, his pigment, his costume—splendid or tattered—but his mind and heart and soul. These are the investment of God in every man. What use man has made of them is another matter; but if God breathed the vital breath into Adam, we have no warrant for thinking it is withheld from any of his sons or that it is stifled even in the most rebellious of his epigoni. If we do not believe that there is an element of grace in every human heart, we cannot love redemptively. "Many tax collectors and sinners came and sat down with Jesus and his disciples." (Matt. 9:10.) Evidently he thought them redeemable; there was a measure of grace in each one to whom his love reached out. This was offensive to the Pharisees, who asked: "Why does your teacher eat with tax collectors and sinners?" (9:11). His answer is familiar: "Go and learn what this means, 'I desire mercy, and not sacrifice.'" Only grace—which is of the same root as gratitude—can respond to mercy and love. To say there was grace in the sinner's heart is not to say he was no sinner; it is to say that it is grace (gratitude) in *every* heart that makes possible a command to love our neighbor, every neighbor, be he saint or sinner.

This is, I believe, what Paul meant when he said: "God shows his love for us in that while we were yet sinners Christ died for us" (Rom. 5:8). The death of Christ would have been futile as a redemptive expedient if there had not been the redeemable core of love in the sinner's heart to which the Cross addresses itself. Grace is a reciprocal operation between God and man, and it is the God in man's heart that makes the love of God's heart operative.

4

There is a further factor in this equation: we are to love our neighbor as we love ourselves. Do we love ourselves? Have we a moral right to self-love? We are told that self-love is sin; here, however, we find it the gauge of our love of another. The self, demanding much, becomes selfishness—the sinister aspect of egotism—demanding little, it diminishes the measure of our love for others—the sinister aspect of self-deprecation.

Escape from this dilemma is to be found in the same way we found inviting above. We love in our neighbor that which is God in him; similarly *we love in ourselves that which is God in us*. This is the way in which we can love ourselves without subtracting from the love that belongs to God. Thus, correctly understood, love of God, of self, and of neighbor are the same thing. The second commandment, to love our neighbor as ourselves, is *like* the first commandment, to love God altogether. This was bringing things new and old out of the storehouse.

Let us not forget what is meant by love. What we can legitimately love in ourselves is not the glowing possessiveness or the often condescending protectiveness of romantic and familial love. It is the grace that is in our own hearts. Here again we find a close identity between love and grace, between the desire to achieve advantage for another and the sense of gratitude in both hearts that makes reciprocal action possible. It is an awesome thing to realize that I have this divine gift, this divine element. Not to love it—and thus love what is God in me—is worse than ingratitude; it is insensitivity.

The concluding lines of Lewis Mumford's book *In the Name of Sanity,* understanding love in a manner similar to its exposition here, say:

> This self-transforming and self-transcending quality of love cannot be called upon for all the little occasions of life, when customary civility and politeness must do duty instead. Part of its magic arises from its freedom and spontaneity, its sudden sense of the occasion, its ability to depart from the expected routine. But when love is genuine, it has the power to open doors that would remain locked and bolted against forceful entry. All over the world, power divorced from love has become insolent, brutal, irrational, and increasingly manic and paranoid; and by those very attributes has become impotent and self-defeating. Now that power has overreached itself, love offers the only alternative that will lead us back to life; the Sermon on the Mount has thus become the new Mount Everest that calls forth the human spirit today. Nothing less than that "impossible" ascent remains as a practical alternative to our yielding to the destructive and inhuman forces that threaten our whole civilization.[2]

5

This may be dismissed, of course, as the *inflatio ad absurdum* of man's self-esteem. From this shimmering summit of

---

[2] (New York: Harcourt, Brace & Co., 1954), pp. 240-41. Used by permission of the author.

pride he is sure to totter and be dashed to ultimate destruction. How certainly is the proud man brought low; how, like the operation of a moral law, he that exalts himself is abased. But what is this self that is abased? This is the nub of the difficulty. Is it God in me, or is it something in me that at war with God arrogates divinity? And yet the exaltation of whatever is in me that is Godlike is not doomed to abasement unless all striving for godliness is a cruel mockery of man's best impulses. If on the contrary it is the exaltation of the qualities that are shall we say human for lack of a better word that is to be frustrated, then at least we can see some moral justification for it. Unless, of course, we believe that man's highest achievement is a successful rebellion against God.

Do we have a right to make so sharp a dichotomy between what in us is God and what is not? Perhaps not, yet this is exactly what has taken place in one way or another in every culture that has been morally and spiritually self-conscious. It is, moreover, the basic justification for pessimism or for optimism. The scientific humanism of a generation ago that reduced man to a colloid of half a dozen chemical elements worth about a dollar and activated by its own conatus was a denial of other spiritual phenomena unique to the human species. It was not surprising that this induced a dismal if not morbid outlook on life and destiny.

This, however, buttered no parsnips; down the ages some spiritually sensitive men have thought of the flesh as evil, worth not a dollar—rather, indeed, a loathsome indebtedness to nature. Asceticism was no answer to this gloomy mood, for the piety that self-denial of this sort produced was tinted by the same somber shades that darkened the picture of the chemical compound.

There is no resolution of the conflict between spirit and body. It is impossible for the finite human mind to decide what in man is of God and what is not. Nor can it rest in the bland confidence that all of man is of God, or in the desperation that none of him is of God. So if we are morally sensitive, we alternate between exultation and despair; we dream splendid dreams and stumble through sticky mud; we blame God and praise ourselves, or praise God and wallow in abnegation. Still it is important that we react to the dilemma; to be unaware of it would mean we were merely creatures of reflexes and instincts; to care nothing about it would mean we had lost or suffocated an inner ember.

Perhaps, after all, it is this awareness that is the ultimate credential of God in us. We shall not resolve the dilemma for the very reason that we are human; we shall not ignore it for the very reason that we are divine. Important to us, however, is the attitude of our Lord. As we have tried to understand his statement of the first and greatest commandment, we have found that it reflects a profound belief in what he saw in man. Think what it means to say that the creative energy of love is a human endowment and that because it is impartially distributed among all the sons of men, all men can be asked to love the divine in themselves, the divine in their neighbors, and—to continue the figure—the divine in God. To make this a command and to give it priority of importance required an act of faith on Jesus' part that is still celestial diameters beyond our puny reach. But that he said it is not to be taken from us and that he made it the base from which operated all the activities of his own creative and redemptive love cannot be convincingly denied.

CHAPTER X

Jesus and People

It is an observed fact of history that its greatest figures seem to stand high, solitary, remote. This is an illusion caused by distance. Not only do the heroic proportions of the renowned seem to dwarf those who stand beside them, but the repetition of the famous name reduces others to anonymity. Furthermore until the beginnings of historical biography a great figure was thought great largely for one reason only: an act of prodigious courage, a revolutionary idea, an invention. This tended further to separate him from his unspectacular fellows. Who remembers the versatility of Socrates: that he was a sculptor of distinction before he became a military hero and then a philosopher? And how many of his friends are known? His associations with a coterie of celebrated Athenians was very important to him, and he was forever thronged by the youth he was accused of corrupting. Yet when we try to recall the names of his friends, Crito, Xenophon, Plato, Critias, and Alcibiades (who became his enemy) are about as far as we can go. Much the same thing is to be said about most other beneficiaries of fame. The fact is, however, that without associates and intimates one does not attain the statuesque proportions of greatness. The long roster of heroes in Hebrews 11 ends thus: "Apart from us they [the heroes] should not be made perfect."

1

In the light of this circumstance it is important to consider the way in which Jesus reacted to people. Fortunately, since the record is simple and deals with the encounter between Jesus and his generation, we know more about his friends than is the case with most of the distinguished personages of antiquity. This is because people were important to him; we encounter him among the folk in and out of homes and villages, by the sea—wherever, indeed, there were people. Temple, agora, market place, saw less of him than the open road, not because he did not have important ideas to expound but because he had human needs to meet, and these and his approach to them furnish us valuable insights into what he thought of man.

Even so the names of his friends are few. His predecessor John, twelve men and the kin of a few of them, two or three women and as many little known men—these have bequeathed to us the familiar names we give our children. There are others who, touched by his healing, were surely his friends—a dozen or so are thus identified. And yet, as was true of the great Athenian, our Lord was the center of throngs who for a while at least, thought of themselves as his friends. Many of them he must have known by name and circumstance. And think for the moment of the billions who over the countless years have discovered that a strong bond has drawn them to one another, namely, the claim that they have been friends of the Galilean.

To us it is important to note that his response to groups and individuals was the same. There is little evidence, if indeed any, that points to a despair of man in the mass. The cynicism that dismisses the mob as a beast with a behavior no intelligent individual would knowingly share or defend seems wholly lacking in Jesus. He saw man in the mass and not infrequently as threatening his person. It is Luke who tells the story of his narrow escape from a Nazareth synagogue congregation that turned into a mob determined to tumble him over a precipice and for no reason except that he had suggested an invidious comparison between his home town and Capernaum. The intention to "throw him down headlong" (Luke 4:29) leaves no doubt as to their murderous fury.

Not only did he know mobs as capricious, hearing him with approbation one moment and shouting him down the next, saluting him as king one morning and calling for his death less than a week later; he also saw the multitudes in subdued and tractable moods: hungry because their intent following had made them improvident of food, patient while their sick were brought to him for healing, elated when the suggestion that he be made king rippled across their surface like a vagrant breeze. Yet he did not describe them as mercurial or menacing or even as malleable. He looked at them as sheep not having a shepherd, as fields of grain white unto the harvest. In the Jordan Valley John had denounced the crowds as a generation of vipers and warned that the ax of doom was already hacking at the root of the tree. Jesus spoke not of doom but of destiny, of the coming of the kingdom of heaven. His news was as good as John's was bad, and the common people heard him gladly. Perhaps the people were mistaken; perhaps he was too much a sentimentalist to assess rightly the crowd mind. Yet the first reference he is reported as making to the crowds who followed him to the place of execution was that it was better to weep for themselves than for him. Few felons on their way to die have shown similar compassion for the curious, the angry, the sadistic, and the morbid who attend such grisly spectacles.

2

His choice of twelve men to compose his intimate inner circle is by any standard odd. Was he naïvely trustful of untrustworthy men; did he think purses could be made out of sow's ears? Can radical differences of temperament be composed into harmony by one man's masterfulness? Here was

Simon, a member of the Zealots, a superpatriotic group militantly irreconcilable to Rome; and Levi, a renegade Jew, hireling of the Roman tax office. How did Jesus expect them to get along together? Or for that matter, was he not inviting unnecessary trouble in bringing the Sons of Thunder—noisy and ambitious for prestige—into fellowship with the dour Thomas or Philip the warrior? No one has yet fully explained the mischoice of Judas—if such it was—and the malapert Peter, and the nonentities who are known only and briefly by name. The spread of the Christian movement obscures its unpromising beginnings, and the occasional indications of tension and estrangement within the twelve cause wonder that there was sufficient cohesion of understanding and purpose to have resulted in anything at all.

Most puzzling to his contemporaries was Jesus' fondness for social outcasts. He was not merely a friend of the underdog, the wretched, and the powerless, on whom so many spray the insecticide of their sympathy. He was a friend of publicans and harlots—sinners. The word "friend" is either carelessly used, or it carries specific intent. The fact that it was used by his ill wishers shows that his contacts with these moral recalcitrants did not look like patronizing or self-flattering condescension. He did not go slumming; he ate with them, abjuring, we may assume, the amenities that respectability prescribed and which his ragamuffin hosts disdained.

He invited guilt by association. To stay with Zacchaeus, the chief tax collector in Jericho, was to incur the odium under which that little man lived. And there are those who have been sure that his fondness for Mary of Magdala is to be understood in simpler terms than the language of soteriology, yet there is no hint of moral obliquity in the record of his life.

It has been customary, of course, to explain this in terms

of his own personal nature; and this is altogether proper. Nevertheless one is not understood in isolation, one does not live in a social vacuum, and a very great deal of what one does is measurably affected by others. Some would say it is wholly determined by others. And part of the way others affect our behavior is due to what we think of them, for we act and react in relation to our own emotional and rational responses to individuals and situations. Our feelings and ideas may be altogether mistaken, but that makes no difference to the fact that we are a part of all that surrounds us.

Thus what Jesus thought of individuals conspicuously affected what he did with them. Again we may say he may have been romantic or ingenuous and thus altogether mistaken. But I do not think he was under any illusions as to the character of the harlot or the publican whose shamelessness both advertised and identified them. It would seem, then, that if he was not deceived by their disreputableness, he must have had reputable reasons for consorting with them. What he thought about them affected what he did with and to them. He was either on a lark or on a mission; either he was blind to their pollution and beguiled by their rebellion, or he knew more deeply the essential good that was hidden beneath their raffish exterior and was challenged to redeem it and set it free.

3

The last few days of his earthly life brought together a compound of human failure, folly, and cowardice such as would have driven most men mad or to a fury of retaliation. How complete was his disillusionment with Simon Peter, we can know only by the name he called him—you Satan—on a familiar occasion. To be repudiated by denial three times repeated and with obscene cursing deserved in our eyes not reprimand but revenge. Yet he allowed it, whatever were his feelings, in silence. Why?

He had had much to say about the blindness and the dishonesty of the religious leaders; but to see them make common cause with political henchmen of the lewd Herod, first to trap him into a seditious remark about taxes, which he skillfully parried, and then to destroy him—how was this to be endured? The combination of ecclesiastical and civil authorities to compel conformity is an ancient evil. Why, instead of conciliating them, did he not let loose a blast of recrimination? This was the combination that tossed him back and forth between them when they had him under judgment. Why did he not denounce their cowardice? Sleepy friends, sprawled in exhaustion under the temporary refuge of olive trees, unable to watch with him one brief hour—what abhorrence this should have caused! Yet he spoke in pity of their weak bodies and commented their willing spirits. Why?

Why was he so silent in the face of his accusers? There are times when there is no use in speaking up; other times when to answer is to excite rather than satisfy a questioner; other times, perhaps, when one is so oppressed by stupidity or malice that silence is a sterner rebuke than words. Pilate asked what truth was, inquiringly or with a sneer. The high priest at his first trial had behaved most indecorously for a judge by tearing his robes in theatrical protest at what he called blasphemy but which was in fact a currently popular slogan from the book of Daniel.

Indignity to his person, we perversely think, he should have accepted without protest. The fascination the synoptists later had in discovering what they regarded as "fulfilled prophecies"—an attestation to the authority of their scriptures and a proof of the uniqueness of the divine appointment of Jesus—somehow makes it easy for us to expect him unprotestingly to endure scourging and death. But by what callousness of heart do we allow him to be spat on, burlesqued as a king by sadistic Roman soldiers, suspected and accused of being a dolt and a destroyer and having all his motives and the record of his ministries shouted down as a menace to the civil, social, and religious orders without seeing it as the monstrous evil it is? Simply because he opened not his mouth. Why then should we even at this late and ineffectual hour open ours?

4

Here emerges an interesting fact: the sufferings of our Lord are generally regarded as a negative response to the evil in the men who slew him; they may have been on the contrary a positive response to the good in men. This takes a good deal of believing, for within our Christian culture the archvillains of all time are the perpetrators of the death of Jesus. The best we can do is to say that a tolerant spirit like his would have said they could not help it; generosity would have said they were doing the best they knew how; despair would have said there is nothing better to be expected from human beings; and vindictiveness would have turned them over to the wrath of God.

Can we believe he endured these compounded insults and indignities because he felt that they were the natural reactions of men to goodness? This would have been an act not of faith but of fatalism. It would, indeed, have been almost a morbid preoccupation with suffering for its own sake—masochism, in modern terms. Men simply do not suffer for causes or institutions or people they deeply believe are futile or polluted or base. They endure hardness for what they believe will pay off—in glory, in coin, in national honor, or whatever. It is quite possible that we do not give the limit ("ye have not yet resisted unto blood" [Heb. 12:4 K.J.V.])

of life and possessions to great causes today because we do not believe they are great and good and demanding of us our all. What was once a glorious career for a soldier, saving the world for democracy—something worth dying for—has become a boring and meaningless acceptance of six months of basic, or two years of service, and six years of reserve status.

Jesus had talked about turning the other cheek. Why? Because he believed it would have restraining and perhaps redemptive effect on the striker. But why did he believe that? Because he believed there was something in the spirit of a man that would respond. We don't turn the other cheek because we think that the spirit of a man is such that he would regard the act as cowardice or weakness and therefore an open road to aggression. If man by nature is depraved, it is palpable folly to treat him as if he can be redeemed. It is only because we can believe that man by nature is good that we can accept the pain, the rebuff, the weariness, the anguish, by which he can be saved from the perversion of his goodness.

On this point Jesus was very positive and very clear. This brings us again to the meaning of love. Love, as we have understood it, is conscious good will toward a fellow being. It is predicated not on active reciprocal good will in others but on the faith that its application even in a hostile situation will *create* good will in others. The opposite of this, of course, is either indifference or vengence; and neither of these moral attitudes can create anything but themselves.

Jesus, who knew what was in man, also knew what man did with what was in him. That a man misuses or even despises the good in himself does not mean that he is inherently base but that he is making base uses of good qualities. Albert Schweitzer said: "Anyone who proposes to do good must not expect people to roll stones out of his way, but must accept his lot calmly if they even roll a few more upon it." Why do they do this ? How can Schweitzer accept this calmly? These are important questions, and reams have been written about them. Our concern, however, is what Jesus had to say.

5

Obviously he undertook nowhere to explain what we call human depravity, and he never referred to the fall of man. Indeed, it is striking to discover that he had very little to say about sin. Only once in the Synoptic Gospels (Matt. 12:31) is the word "sin" used in its singular form. Even here "every sin" is the equivalent of "all sins" and thus plural in meaning, but this comes nearer to a generic use of the word than any other in the record. He was named Jesus because he was to "save his people from their sins" (Matt. 1:21); he was asked by Peter how often he should forgive a brother who sinned against him (Matt. 18:21); the episode of his anointing by the woman in the house of Simon the leper shows the Pharisees skeptical of his right to forgive sin and his clear assumption of the responsibility. In so flagrant a case as hers he could not romanticize her behavior. "Her sins, which are many, are forgiven." But his approach to her was less along the negative line of condemnation than the positive line of commendation. "She loved much," said Jesus; and to the woman he said: "Your faith has saved you."

This cannot be taken to mean that he was unaware of sin or casual in its treatment. He had come to save his people from their sins. It must be allowed, then, that one way he did it was by recognizing saving qualities people have in themselves—love and faith, for example. Why, we may ask, did the Samaritan woman forget her jar at the well, hurry back to her village, and tell the astonishing news that she had encountered a man who told her everything she had ever done? Everything? What an opportunity for the village gossips to fill in gaps of information about her lurid past that they had only been able to guess at! It is hard to account for this woman's enthusiasm except by assuming that this mild-mannered traveler at Jacob's well had told her some *good* things she had done. This was exciting to one with so tarnished a reputation as hers. Little wonder she speculated as to the possibility of his being the Messiah.

While our Lord spoke sparingly about sin, he had much to say about that magic quality in men that is called faith. He marveled at it in some; he commented on its potency in others; he deplored its weakness where it was aggressed by despondency or danger. Did everyone have it? Centurion, Syrophoenician woman, the paralytic's four friends, the harlot in Simon's house, servants, masters, stewards—these had faith. Bartimaeus, the blind beggar, had enough to cure his blindness. Faith that could cleanse a harlot and restore sight to a blind man and healing to a paralytic—this was a human quality to talk about indeed.

Righteousness was another familiar word with him though used less frequently. Even the Pharisees had something that passed for it—low grade, perhaps, to be exceeded by all those who were concerned with godliness. It was something easy to imitate, and its counterfeit had to be discounted, but it turned up in strange places. Those in the great assize (Matt. 25:31) who are called righteous were most surprised to discover that the acts of kindness that had won them the name and the eternal reward had been performed on God, incarnate in the sick, the hungry, the naked, and the imprisoned.

6

That Jesus could be fierce in his denunciation of human wickedness is given ample illustration in his excoriation of the scribes and Pharisees. What was their over-all sin? It needs, of course, to be said that though Jesus did not discourse about sin *qua* sin, he identified "sins" with sharp discernment and talked about them. The range is wide. Hypocrisy is the most obvious illustration, but the gamut runs all the way from dishonesty to fruitlessness. The stupid shortsightedness of the house built on sand, the nonchalant improvidence of the five foolish virgins, the pride that put servant above master, the blind perversity that would not dance to gaiety or weep to sorrow, the equivocation that could not take sides against evil, the presumption that impugned motives—these represent the target of his rebuke. The much misunderstood "unpardonable sin" (a deliberate identification of God as evil, of falsehood as truth); the hidden malice in intemperate or careless talk; the faithlessness that demanded proof (sign) of the unprovable; the devotion to dead traditions; the stubborn refusal to forgive and exercise mercy toward the penitent; hardness of heart, avarice, ruthless ambition—even for "good" positions—laziness, rudeness (the wedding garment)—each of these will suggest the episode in which he confronted it. We will incline to regard many of them as belonging in the hazy area between sin and error, between malice and folly, between deliberate act and awkwardness. Such classifications have been attempted; note the mortal and venial sins of Roman Catholic morality and the spacious range between the two where common sense (tradition) allows moral improvisation and compromise. The point, however, is clear: Jesus' awareness of human defections from the purpose and law of God was profound, but it did not rest on a hypothesis concerning the congenital corruption of the spirit.

To him there was a basic sin; it was hypocrisy—which is dishonesty. The deliberate lie is the basis of all immorality, and by the same token honesty is the apex of all virtues. But for all we speak about congenital liars, a lie that is congenital is no lie at all since it is not a calculated and determined effort to deceive. The evil aspect of mendacity is that it is indulged by one who knows the truth. Jesus made this clear as he denounced the religious leaders. They deliberately stood as a barrier to the kingdom of heaven while they invited wayfarers in; they deliberately corrupted the proselyte whose innocence they had exploited; they—who *could* see—were deliberately blind lest they *should* see.

It is not necessary to continue the indictment. The point is, however, that hypocrisy is a perversion of goodness; it is a use of what is good in such a way as to achieve evil ends. And that is not possible except to one who knows what the good is or has an inherent aptitude for it. The tragedy of life, as we within the Christian tradition know it, is not in disappointment or defeat or even the fact of death itself. It lies in the denial of what is good within the heart, the natural response to need, the suffocation of the living dream, the repudiation of the awareness that makes another's wrong, or privation, or perdition, one's own. This is not tragedy in the Greek tradition in which the defeat of the protagonist of good is the core of the narrative intention, and the causes of his destruction are innate in the personality or the circumstances he is powerless to change. He dies heroically as his final act of defiance of his immitigable fate. What is innate in Christian man is not his doom; it is his destruction of the good he knows is in him that is his ruin. This is his sin from which he is saved by divine grace, unlike his Greek counterpart who, the victim of remorseless fate, knows no redemption this side of Elysium.

7

What were the qualities that Jesus saw in man that gave him his unique character and furnished the elements out of which he was to be made into the likeness of God? We say *be made* rather than *make himself* because it is the assumption that he can make himself into the form of Godliness that is his most subtle antagonist. From our survey of the language of the Master we have come upon three words: faith, love, and honesty. They do not all appear in these common forms except perhaps the first. We cannot escape the word "honesty" any more than he was able to escape it in those he encountered.

Faith: this is a posture of the spirit; it always leans forward. Sometimes ever so slightly—"O men of little faith"—sometimes bent as to press full strength against a mighty barrier —and a mountain is cast into the sea. This human endowment has nothing to do with right and wrong. Perhaps the mountain should be left where it is, but it is under the spur of faith that man is impelled toward what at the moment he thinks desirable. "Without faith it is impossible to please [God]." Love is clearly what has been said all along—the compassionate impulse, the will to good, calculated good will. This, whether in the social discard who broke a vase of nard over him, or in the Samaritan giving first aid to a robber victim, or in the hosts before the Great Throne who had befriended the needy because of an inner compulsion they could not restrain—this was an authentic, inexpungeable spiritual quality that all the sons of men had.

Honesty? The word is not used, but it is vividly present in much that he said about hypocrisy. There is no substitute for sincerity, no moral alternative to being real. For to be real is to be free. We are to worship in spirit and in truth, which means with enthusiasm and sincerity. Worship and worshiper are real only when they are sincere just as all worthy work is worthful less in the perfection of its product than in the fidelity of the craftsman to what is real in his craft. And the same thing is to be said about art. All we can ask of the artist is sincerity. It is obvious that Jesus believed and saw in man this urgency toward the real, call it reality, fidelity, sincerity, honesty, or what not. Were this not in the heart of man, he would have built no permanent culture; for his indifference to reality or his preoccupation with fraud and falsity would have inhibited or falsified all his strivings. And it is because man has this in himself that he can be made to see the emptiness of pride and the shame of folly and the folly of sin.

It took all three of these qualities in himself to cope with the multifarious problems of human stupidity and mischief. None has denied that he had them in superlative measure; none can properly deny that his faith and gentleness must have often been sorely tried. "Faithless and perverse generation, . . . how long am I to bear with you?" (Matt. 17:17.) And it would seem to follow that it was because he believed them to be hidden even in the darkest heart that he was willing to risk the venture of redemption. Any other understanding of man would seem to have made the whole of his life an unreasoning defiance of fact, at best the quixotic experiment of a dreamer, at worst the stubborn folly of a fool. But we call him Redeemer and Lord, and we do well.

8

To follow the record we have of the last anguished hours of his life is to see the ultimate demonstration of his faith in man. We allow ourselves the luxury of forgiveness if our assailant is sufficiently contrite or abject. This is what made George Bernard Shaw say that forgiveness is condescension and he wanted none of it. But what of the forgiveness that is offered even while indignity is being suffered? Despite the fact that some specialists have warned us that the words uttered on the cross may have the work of late copyists, it is nonetheless manifest that even if this were true, something in the character of the dying Christ made such emendations both credible and reassuring. Why, we ask, did he forgive those who were doing him to death? Was it the heroism of the protagonist who defies the fate that destroys him? Was it the sentimentalism of one who had put too high a value on man? Heinrich Heine, famous German poet, said: "I, too, might have died for men if I had not the suspicion that they were not worth it." Or was it the confidence of the lover of humankind who was releasing in a memorable and creation-shaking word the very energy of redemption itself? The answer is that he knew what was in man and was moving out to meet it, even through the deepening shadows that gathered to attest his mortal end.

CHAPTER XI

Summary and Conclusion

There was something in the elevation of the mind of Jesus that gave freshness, vigor, and clarity to his thinking about man. Like the slow diffusion of the air of the mountain descending to the humid flats, stirring the torpid heat and driving it aloft for cooling, so he brought to the listless or despondent mind of his generation reassurances that revived and heartened it. His was hardly a happy age; people lived without very much hope. Too often they had been disillusioned by the failures of pretenders, and the promise of a return of the golden days of David had worn thin with endless iteration. Indeed, it was in many ways a cruel world. Empire at times must provide bread and circuses for the people's amusement but more practically for its own protection against revolt. Most of the time, however, it is ruthless and contemptuous of the innermost longings of the human heart. Add to the cruelty of imperial dominion the depressed living standards brought about by crushing taxation.

Yet there were some good and wise men, serious pagans who, disavowing religion because it had become largely superstition, exercised their concern for humanity by writing humane treatises on life and destiny. Why is it that such men did not succeed in shaping or remaking the world of their time? Why did not men follow them and create a new culture? Why did the moral impact of their wit and gentleness die with the death of their empire? A. C. Bouquet says:

> They did not hold out any real hope of transforming the world in which they lived into a better place, and only offered people one of two alternatives, either how to school themselves to bear

the unhappiness of their existence with stern fortitude, or how to escape out of that existence into another and less perishable one.[1]

How unlike Jesus that sounds. "Stern fortitude" is a different beatitude from rejoicing and being exceeding glad in suffering. To assert the fact of the kingdom of heaven and the promise of its wider fulfillment was something even his friend Peter was to learn long after his famous sermon in which his final exhortation was: "Save yourselves from this crooked generation" (Acts 2:40).

People came to follow the Christians not only because they seemed to offer a more substantial hope for the future, by making the name of Deity more than an empty phrase, and by insisting he had a purpose for the world, but also because they seemed able to transform society by persuasion rather than by force, and to make it gentler, kinder, and juster; and all this on the basis of fact, and not myth or fantasy.

Purpose and fact are the important words in this quotation. Purpose, as we have been looking at it in the words of Jesus, is at least partially contained in the phrase "the kingdom of heaven." Fact, as we have discovered it, is partially the confidence in themselves that Jesus gave his followers, thus enabling them to participate in the divine enterprise.

1

This confidence was, we may believe, the result of what Jesus saw in man and the way he identified himself with man. Our important emphasis on Jesus as the incarnation of God must not obscure our understanding of him as the incarnation of man. It is this latter fact that has been sketched

[1] *Everyday Life in New Testament Times* (New York: Chas. Scribner's Sons, 1953), p. 3.

in these studies. We see what man is by looking at man's noblest Son, even as we see what God is in the same way.

Man senses his innate powers and is tempted to use them in ways that destroy the integrity of physical, social, and moral laws. No man lives who is not aware of power, and no man indulges power without risks that determine his destiny. This is the story of the temptation experience in the wilderness solitude in which Jesus was clearly identifying himself with the normal human struggle.

The Beatitudes boldly identify salt and light as qualities of the human spirit, qualities that imply the capacity for rightness and an imperious hunger and thirst for it, plus an aptitude for the satisfaction of the splendid appetency.

Confronting the moral absolutes that forbid killing an adversary (murder), violating his integrity (adultery), or traducing his reputation by false witness, Jesus posits a measure of inner discipline that can intercept these evil acts as they arise as anger, lust, and deception in the heart. And dealing with the absolutes of the religious experience—the giving of one's self, the replenishment of one's spirit, and the ritual disciplines of piety, symbolized by alms, prayer, and fasting—he pointed out not only that all men yield to these impulses but that they also corrupt them by masquerade, the wish to be seen of men—in a word, hypocrisy.

Outside the concern of moral and religious practices there lies the spacious area within which behavior is under neither religious nor moral compulsions. It has been called the area where common sense is the monitor of conduct. The law imposes no penalty nor does religious censure fall upon deviation from what have been accepted as decorous and rational standards. Man is an insatiable seeker after values. His quest for light sometimes lands him in darkness, and nothing is more frightening than to think that darkness is light. He is aware of the value of loyalties that protect and enrich him, but he will discomfit himself in the tensions created by trying to serve God and mammon. And yet if in the concern for inner integrity he chooses one primary loyalty, he must choose rightly. The Gentiles pursue food, drink and shelter with relentless concentration. The result: anxiety.

Again, man's sense of values makes him pass judgment on his fellows. Nothing that characterizes the human spirit is more precious than his critical faculty. Conversely, when it is used censoriously (mote and beam) and dishonestly (hypocrite), it not only loses its essential usefulness; it becomes the agent of hostility. So common sense instructs man not to misuse the values of the spirit by giving them to dogs or the values of things (pearls) by casting them before swine. Holy things and beautiful things are provided for the human spirit; it alone can sense and protect their worth. Laughter and love and beauty are not for dogs and swine; yet man, who has the capacity to assess their worth for himself, can also commit the folly of discarding them carelessly or in rebellious anger.

2

While Jesus responded to a request for his opinion on men's primary moral obligation in terms of law and religion —the law and the prophets—he still set his reply within the categories of a sort of *quid pro quo* common sense. When men today think of the Golden Rule, it is less in terms of law and piety than in terms of its practical pay-off. Indeed, it is not uncommon to hear men who are ostentatiously nonreligious—or even, we hazard to say, little concerned with law—claim that this radiant maxim is the rule of their lives.

How far below the level of formal law and prescribed religious piety this reaches is seen when we discover that the assumption on which this rule rests is the aptitude for mutuality that seems to characterize all living things. Mutuality is not a response to moral obligations that nature knows nothing of. The limited mutuality or even its phases which to us seem to be hostility (self-preservation) or individuality (non-co-operation) cannot be called right or wrong in naturalistic terms. It is simple observable common sense that regards a recognition and extension of this existent mutuality as the best way to get along. Religiously, to be sure, we say that this means every living thing is partner with God in a universal enterprise. Philosophically we would perhaps says it indicates that everything is in rational correspondence with everything else. Sociologically there is no little ground for saying that this was essential to survival for human primitives, and comradeship between lower animals and men was something that the refinements of civilization have unhappily diminished. We think of the Golden Rule as applicable in human relations only, but is it unlikely that it can operate there unless it can be thought operative in all life form? The narrow gate as the symbol of man's need and ability for a concentration of his energies instead of a careless diffusion of them; the identity of tree and fruit—we call this the proper relation of ends and means—the establishment of the "house" of one's life on the firm rock of performance instead of the insubstantial sand of bombast—these are further indications that Jesus in the name of common sense and without a syllable of threat believed that there was something in the nature of the human spirit that would respond to his good-tempered and sometimes even humorous admonitions. He knew that they would be totally unheeded by some and often forgotten by all. In such circumstances the consequences would irreversibly follow: the tension, the anxiety, the hostility, the waste, the indecision, the disillusion, and sometimes the whole house crashing under the intermittent assaults of wind and rain. But man, who can very largely avert disaster, will also assign the cause for it when he is overwhelmed. He may indulge in self-pity or in pointless accusations, but even these perverse moods are an inverse witness to the capacity for weighing values that is indigenous to his psyche.

It is this that confronts us with the value-relation involved in ends and means, or as it is put, the relation between grapes and thistles, or wolves in sheep's clothing. This has been moralized, and properly so, making a harmony between means and end the rudiment of moral integrity. But before religion or law demanded it, common sense prescribed it; and it is common sense that today holds tenaciously to it when law and religion let it fall from their lifeless hands.

3

Man is what he is partly by his nature and partly by his association with others. He has power to associate himself with others. It is called gregariousness. Often society confuses him by asking of him certain attitudes and acts that are distasteful. The tension between him and the aggregate of his fellows may torture him or teach him ways of composing conflicts. It is this capacity for community (it is called mutuality above) that makes possible the growth of cultures. Haphazard, perhaps; or by his response to challenge; or in the language of Jesus the pursuit of the kingdom of heaven —a concept of a social experience that men can share as a treasure, a dream, a growing tree, a yeasty ferment, and a net that is cast into the sea.

Central to this, of course, is the assumption that man can be drawn to his neighbor by love, even as he is drawn to God. Hence man must love God exclusively. If then he is to love his neighbor, he must love that in his neighbor which is God; and if he is to love himself, he can love only that in himself which is God. It is impossible to comprehend man's relation to himself, his God, and his neighbor in more profound and exalted terms.

This is at least suggestive of the perspectives within which Jesus looked at man. It is not the whole picture; there are elements—the apocalyptic, for example—that seem to lie outside this wider view; but they do not falsify or contradict the essence of his faith in human nature. This does not mean that he was quixotic or sentimental. He saw man's sin deepened by vainglory, avarice, and folly; and no one was ever more stern than he in his denunciation of the hypocrisy that made a compound of all three. Yet it was because he believed in men that he warned them, because he loved men that he pled with them, because he hoped in men that he forgave them. His faith in his betrayer was justified by Judas' desperate retributory suicide; his hope for his executioners was steadied by his dying prayer for their exculpation.

4

It is perhaps enough to try to state the case; to account for it leads into speculations insufficiently sustained by the biblical record. There may be reason for thinking that the religious faith of his people was predominantly hopeful. The lyric poetry of its literature was gay; the epic poetry uniformly ended with a testimony of praise. When national fortunes were low, the dream of a restoration of the glories of David or of a new Zion penciled the clouds with a fringe of light. Indeed, it is to be expected that a people who hoped in the Lord would not be given over to despair of their own ultimate destiny.

Nevertheless we do not explain the mind of Jesus altogether or even largely by the *Zeitgeist* of the Jews in the first century or by the sacred lore he treasured in his heart. Least of all can we dismiss him as one who by refusing to look at life was able to be satisfied by delusions and fantasies.

We must be content with the comment of the author of the Fourth Gospel, a judgment that seems to reflect his surprise as much as his admiration: "He himself knew what was in man."[2] Add to this the criterion by which he constantly formed his own judgments: "You will know them by their fruits." If this strikes us as theologically naïve, we need only to recall what the Pharisees thought when he said that publicans and sinners would precede them into the kingdom of heaven. That was not naïveté; it was sacrilege!

To return to this estimate of human nature today is theologically offbeat. The central stress of neo-orthodoxy derives from its return to the paleo-orthodoxy of Augustine, Luther, and Calvin.[3] It is interesting that it does not go further back. Augustine, of course, *did* go back—to Paul—and accepted from him one idea of man that fitted his own experience. I say *one* idea because Paul is clearly ambiguous. The twelfth chapter of Romans is difficult, if not impossible, to reconcile with his famous lament in verses 21-25 of the seventh chapter in which he describes his own inner conflict without extrapolating it to humanity in general. Not that we all do not feel much the same about ourselves much of the time; but it is not safe to enlarge private, subjective feelings to universal dimensions. If man is always as impotent as he sometimes feels, then to exhort him, for example, to "repay no one evil for evil, but take thought for what is noble in the sight of all" (Rom. 12:17) is as unavailing as writing in water.

Discussed at some length in Chapter II was the relation of the sense of power to the essential nature of man. It is this rather than innocence with which he was originally endowed in the Genesis story. Access to wisdom—not wisdom

[2] Cf. comment on p. 6.
[3] Cf. Arnold S. Nash, ed., *Protestant Thought in the Twentieth Century* (New York: The Macmillan Co., 1951), pp. 131-32.

itself—was offered our primal parents. It was power that set the stage for the experience of Jesus in the wilderness story. He demonstrated that power is available for good and evil uses, for the support of the integrity of physical, social, and moral or for their repudiation. And as representative man, intuitively aware of and responsive to the divine will, he chose to use his power divinely. So also must all men.

The emphasis of Augustine on man's corrupt nature has no explicit support in what we know of Jesus' teaching. It therefore raises two questions. Was not the bishop's preoccupation with what has come to be known as original sin due to his own "tormented" (his own word) life? Hurried, as he was in his polemical writings, into extreme positions respecting the absoluteness of divine grace and the absoluteness of human corruption, he repeated, albeit in extreme terms, the eccentric experience of Paul. David Smith, a cautious and conservative scholar, suggests that the torment of the great apostle may have been the same "body of death" that burdened the life of Augustine.[4]

The second question raised by Augustinianism—as it is generally understood—is whether man, if he is essentially evil due to his physical generation by an act that is inherently evil, could *know* his sinfulness. That man thinks he is good is evidence, we are told, of his corrupt nature. If, however, his nature is corrupt, are not his critical faculties corrupt? Is he not innately unable to make correct judgments about

[4] *The Life and Letters of St. Paul* (New York: George H. Doran Co., 1920), p. 31, 33: "Here [I Cor. 14:34], with a reticence which evinces the painfulness of the confession, the veil is half lifted from a dark episode of those unrecorded years. What precisely it may have been is unrevealed, and surmise were banal. . . . The confession, however, should not be attenuated. In a nature so ardent and impulsive there are ever tragic possibilities; and it is no marvel that his soul should have been swept by a gust of passion and defiled by a deed of impurity. . . . And in view of the sternness of his attitude toward women it would seem as though there were here a hidden tragedy and a bitter memory." (Cf. Rom. 7:7-11.) Used by permission of Harper & Brothers.

anything? When he judges himself to be sinful, how are we to know that *that* judgment is untainted by his inner pollution?

Paul said it was the Law that taught him the powerlessness of the will to achieve righteousness. But, one may ask, what taught him the *power* of the will? God's grace in Christ gave him the victory over weakness and sin, but this was not done by depriving him of his own power of choice.

5

What I am saying is that a return to the experience of Jesus as he endured the vicissitudes of mortality gives us a different picture from that presently exhibited by neo-orthodoxy. "The real essence of sin is man's willful (albeit often unconscious) rebellion against the sovereignty of God and the effort to organize his universe of values around himself as the center." There can hardly be a simpler or more accurate statement of the case. But the base on which it rests is man's power to will, to rebel, and to organize. He may use his power to conform as well as to rebel, to confuse as well as to organize; and the influences that impel his choices are varied. His will is not an evil will; it is a will that can be good or bad. Paul was surely speaking in an excess of despair when he said, "I do not do the good I want, but the evil I do not want is what I do" (Rom. 7:19). Why then was he writing to the Romans? Was it good he did not want to do or evil he was compelled to do?

It is on this matter that we think the guidance of Jesus is clearer. As he saw man, he was a creature uniquely endowed with power. This is the essence of Godlikeness. We talk of God as being good—in terms of love—or bad—in terms of justice. These are not absolute moral categories; they are adaptations that the finite human mind must make. We combine love and justice because we must, but humanely speaking we regard love as a greater personal good than justice. Therefore when we think of God as power, absolute, transcendent, sovereign, we tend to garnish his power with attitudes that favor our limited sense of power. And Godliness in us is the use of the power with which we are endowed in accordance with God's will for his creation.

To go back, as neo-orthodoxy properly insists, to the absolute, transcendent sovereignty of God must not take us to the point where man is evacuated of his sense of meaning, dignity, and responsibility that derives from his awareness of power. If God's will is absolutely transcendent, it can brook no relative rival will. This dilemma is not to be escaped; it is the ancient problem of freedom and authority. But to take away man's sense of power is to destroy him. To renounce power is to destroy one's self. "O to be nothing, nothing," as an old hymn asks, is less Christian than Buddhist.

Man's essential nature, Jesus felt, was Godlike in origin; his destiny is established by the creative purpose and sustained by the creative power. What God is doing is therefore more important than what man is doing; and the moment man reverses that order of importance, he commits the original (not congenital) sin. The divine-human encounter should be a creative partnership of the powers of God and man. If it were wholly God's, man's existence would be denatured of freedom and power; if it were wholly man's, it would forfeit divine guidance. On this assumption our Lord based his instructions to his friends. He could not have urged them to let their light shine if he had thought the light in them was darkness. He would hardly have challenged them to bear their crosses if he had secretly felt that cross-bearing was beyond the limits of human strength.

The fact of man's potential is not to be confused with the gauge of his power. Man's use of power is often little above the level of weakness. This means that, however sound may be man's power-health quotient, he is often very sick. He is, in other words, a sinner. He is impotent to exercise his full power; he must constantly draw on the reserves of others and of God. He will fall into panic that enervates him because of situations within and without that overwhelm him; but he will also on occasion rise to prodigies of achievement, within and without, and, we hope, give God the glory. This is what Jesus promised his friends. Fear not, he said; greater works shall you do. And his final word rings in the memory like a persistent bell: "You shall receive power when the Holy Spirit has come upon you; and you shall be my witnesses . . . to the end of the earth" (Acts 1:8). One may be allowed to speculate as to what would have happened to the Christian enterprise if it had been initiated with a less reassuring note. Perhaps the surprising thing about man is that he behaves as well as he does and that he will at terrific cost to himself keep on caring, and working, and sacrificing, and dying for the things he believes he has been given power to win and cherish.

6

Such criticism of current theological positions as has been voiced here rests largely on the fact that they are not biblically supported. This does not mean that they have no support from the sacred record. It has been pointed out many times that almost any notion—absurb or sublime—can find a verse somewhere to corroborate it. Our difficulty is to avoid selectivity. Who does? Who can? But the intention of this survey of the mind of Jesus is once again to set it forth at a time when it has become popular to be pessimistic about man. We have happily passed out the blinding radiance of the optimism of an earlier period of Christian thought; and subdued light, or even heavy shadow, is easier on our eyes. But darkness is blindness even as the excess of light. Furthermore we must reserve the right to dismiss the judgment of our Lord on human nature as mistaken. It is not as easy as once it was to find existential support for it. If we do, then we must go on to a more plausible understanding of man and act upon it. Where this will take us, we cannot fully know; but where Jesus' knowledge of man took him is the central confidence of the whole Christian testimony.

Today our self-esteem and reliance on established institutions are unsteadied by the convulsions of our times. Doubting ourselves we doubt others, and suspicion builds barriers behind which to brew the bitter broth of fear. It is when the tempers of men are hot with anger and the hearts of men are inflamed with mistrust that there is need for a cooling wind to lift the heavy air and suffuse our low levels with freshness. Subdued to ears grown weary of the din, reassuring to hearts long daunted by peril, and healing to spirits broken by defeat, the breath from the mountain descends, sometimes soundless, sometimes whispering, sometimes speaking, sometimes crying aloud, but always saying: "Behold, I have given you authority to tread upon serpents and scorpions, and over all the power of the enemy; and nothing shall hurt you. Nevertheless do not rejoice in this, that the spirits are subject to you; but rejoice that your names are written in heaven." (Luke 10:19-20.)

"And when Jesus finished these sayings, the crowds were astonished at his teaching, for he taught them as one who had authority, and not as their scribes." (Matt. 7:28-29.)